Wh
an Atheist
& Other Works

Why I Am an Atheist

& Other Works

With a New Introduction by **S. IRFAN HABIB**

BHAGAT SINGH

VINTAGE

An imprint of Penguin Random House

VINTAGE

Vintage is an imprint of the Penguin Random House group of companies whose addresses can be found at global.penguinrandomhouse.com

Published by Penguin Random House India Pvt. Ltd
4th Floor, Capital Tower 1, MG Road,
Gurugram 122 002, Haryana, India

Penguin
Random House
India

First published in Penguin Books by Penguin Random House India 2023
This edition published in Vintage by Penguin Random House 2024

Copyright © Bhagat Singh 2021

10 9 8 7 6 5 4 3 2 1

The views and opinions expressed in this book are the author's own and the facts are as reported by him which have been verified to the extent possible, and the publishers are not in any way liable for the same.

Please note that no part of this book may be used or reproduced in any manner for the purpose of training artificial intelligence technologies or systems.

ISBN 9780143462262

Typeset in Minion Pro by Manipal Technologies Limited, Manipal
Printed at Replika Press Pvt. Ltd, India

www.penguin.co.in

MIX
Paper | Supporting
responsible forestry
FSC™ C016779

Contents

Introduction

A Memorable Legacy of Revolutionary Ideas

Few names among our galaxy of freedom fighters evoke as much widespread respect and awe as Bhagat Singh's. Remarkably, he achieved this in a brief life of just twenty-three years.

Most of us revere him as a martyr, a status he certainly deserves, but this is an incomplete veneration of the man who left behind a profound revolutionary legacy. Bhagat Singh envisioned an intellectually and institutionally revamped post-Independence India, a dream he intensely cherished during his short life. The essay 'Why I Am an Atheist' is a testament, which culminated into an essay, was born out of fierce engagement with ideas, books, films, plays and, of course, the politics of the times.

Before delving into the essay, it will be useful to comprehend the evolution of Bhagat Singh as a thinker that finally led him to write this enormously powerful essay.

He began thinking and writing at a young age, inheriting this legacy from his family. He also had an advantage of being born in a family of committed nationalists, who were also thinking people. For example, his grandfather, Sardar Arjun Singh, defied Sikh beliefs by planting tobacco in his village, taking advantage of the fertile soil known for its suitability for cultivation.

He faced boycott and criticism from his community, but he did not budge. After selling his crop, he sought pardon by explaining the logic behind his action. Bhagat Singh learnt from his family to fight with courage against the superstitious beliefs through logic-based protest. His uncle, Ajit Singh, who was involved with the peasantry, led a farmer's protest movement in Punjab, maybe the first organized one in India. His other uncle, Swaran Singh, spent several years in prison and died young of tuberculosis. Bhagat Singh's father, Sardar Kishan Singh, was a Congressman, who spent several years in British prisons. With this background, it was no surprise that his first journalistic piece appeared in 1924 in a Hindi magazine called *Matwala*. This article was on 'Universal Brotherhood', a difficult subject to write for a young boy of seventeen. An article like 'Why I Am an Atheist', written just four years later in 1930–31, shouldn't surprise us. His two years in prison exposed him to diverse scholarship, ranging from politics, economics, sociology, philosophy to various genres of poetry and fiction. His journey towards rational thinking and the courage to question everything, as I said before, began early in his life.

If we know this background, then it is not difficult to explain why he was able to think and write so profoundly about the complex social, philosophical, economic and political issues. Being a voracious reader, Bhagat Singh read anything that helped him to unravel the complexities of life, from both prose as well as poetry.

All his comrades reported in their memoirs that they never saw Bhagat Singh without a book in his hand and a few in his pockets. Even his mother reprimanded him for pushing books into his jacket pockets, which were mostly torn. He was also passionate about some meaningful as well as romantic films, with *Uncle Tom's Cabin* being his favourite. He learnt a lot from the plays he participated in as a young man.

When one talks about him as a thinking individual and not just as a raw nationalist, it does not imply that he was a scholar in his teens. It only indicates that he had a profound engagement with world literature through intense reading during his short life. It is also an attempt to bring out his real persona and wean him away from his image of a trigger-happy young man. An image deliberately publicized by the colonial government, which many of us internalized and continue to romanticize every day. We know he lived a short life, most of which was spent under the surveillance of the colonial government. Yet, he could pursue his passion of reading and writing relentlessly.

Before his arrest after the Delhi Assembly bombing on 8 April 1929, Bhagat Singh was associated with the Punjabi monthly called *Kirti* (Worker) during 1928. Sohan Singh Josh, leader of the Kirti Kisan Party from Amritsar, invited him to join the editorial board. Before I come to the essay 'Why I Am an Atheist', it will be useful to briefly track the insightful writings of Bhagat Singh in *Kirti* that will surely help us understand the intellectual evolution and progress in his thinking.

I will refer to two articles that are central to the seminal essay we are concerned with here. These two pieces were written for the June 1928 issue of *Kirti*. They were titled 'Achoot ka Sawaal' (On Untouchability) and 'Sampradayik Dange aur Unka Ilaj' (Communal riots and their solutions). These two articles, as I said before, categorically convey the trajectory that finally led Bhagat Singh to write a more politically mature and philosophically profound essay called 'Why I Am an Atheist'.

What he wrote in 1928 appears to be contemporaneous even now, which unfortunately proves how little has been done to resolve these questions. In the first piece, Bhagat Singh starts by saying, 'Our country is in a really bad shape; here, the strangest questions are asked, but the foremost among them concerns the Untouchables, who account for six crores in a population of thirty crores. For instance, would contact with an untouchable mean defilement of an upper caste? Would the Gods in the temples not get angry by the entry of untouchables? . . . That these questions are being asked in the twentieth century, is a matter which makes us hang our heads in shame.'[1] He questioned the claims we make that we were a great civilization and spiritually superior when he wrote:

> We Indians boast of our spiritualism, but then, we avoid accepting every human being as a fellow being just like ourselves. Western people on the other hand, who bear the reputation of being money-minded, have unequivocally affirmed their faith in the principle of equality. This they

[1] S. Irfan Habib, ed. *Inquilab: Bhagat Singh on Religion and Revolution*, Yoda Press and Simon & Schuster, New Delhi, 2023, p. 18.

did during the revolutions in America and France and above all in Russia; these days Russia is committed to the extension of this principle to all aspects of life, and to ending discriminations in any form whatsoever . . .[2]

He did not stop here but went ahead in confronting and castigating the discriminatory practices, contrasting our regressive socio-political world with the changes being reported from various Euro-American countries. He continued:

'But we Indians who never tire of boasting about our gods and godliness are, even now seriously debating whether to permit untouchables to wear the sacred thread or the janeu, and whether untouchables should be permitted to read the Vedas/Shastras. We often complain about our maltreatment in other countries, and particularly when we are maltreated by the whites, but do we have any moral right to voice such a protest?'[3]

These are all worrisome questions that confront us even now, Bhagat Singh had the courage and foresight to engage with them even before Independence.

As a young writer, just out of his teens, Bhagat Singh was profoundly stirred by the communal upsurge of the 1920s. Expressing his anguish in the second article, he held some of the political leaders and the press responsible for inciting communalism. He believed that 'there were a few sincere leaders, but their voice is easily

---

[2] Ibid. p. 18.
[3] Ibid.

swept away by the rising wave of communalism. In terms of political leadership, India had gone totally bankrupt'.

Bhagat Singh felt that journalism used to be a noble profession, which had now fallen from grace. Now they give bold and sensational headlines to incite people to kill each other in the name of religion. There were riots at several places simply because the local press behaved irresponsibly and indulged in rabble-rousing through their articles. Not much seems to have changed since Bhagat Singh wrote these lines. He categorically spelt out the duties of journalists and then also accused them of dereliction of this duty. He wrote thus:

> 'The actual duty of newspapers is to educate, to liberate people from narrow-mindedness, eradicate fundamentalism, to help in creating a sense of fraternity among people, and to build a common nationalism in India, but these papers behaved in a manner entirely antithetical to their duties. Their sole motive was to spread hysteria, preach narrow-mindedness, fundamentalism, instigate clashes and destroy the common heritage of India.'[4]

Not much seems to have changed since Bhagat Singh wrote this several decades ago. This categorical indictment of the press from an iconic nationalist like Bhagat Singh should be an eye-opener for those in the media today, who are busy dividing people in the name of nationalism, religion, caste and culture.

It will be enlightening to put on record an important episode in the intellectual journey of Bhagat Singh.

---

[4] Ibid. p. 14.

Before the Assembly bomb explosion in April 1929, the revolutionaries stayed at Agra for some time and set up a small office at Hing ki Mandi. Bhagat Singh soon established a small library, comprising 175 books by around seventy authors. Most of them collected from his friends and supporters. Though small, the library was rich in literature, mainly comprising books on economics. There were also books on trade union movement, explosives and bomb-making, and few about the life-sketch of Russian revolutionaries. These books are still lying in a state of neglect at Maalkhana Record in a lower trial court of Lahore. His essay 'Why I Am an Atheist' is a culmination of this intellectual and political journey that began from his childhood and ended with his martyrdom.

His intellectual life really got a boost after his arrest, though he was already an avid reader. Shiv Verma, one of his close comrades in jail, wrote about his love for books thus: 'We had easy access to books in the jail since the day one and the atmosphere was quite congenial for study and exchange of ideas . . . but Bhagat Singh's arrival made this livelier . . . Though we all had a passion for reading, but Bhagat Singh was a class by himself. Despite his soft corner for socialism, he was passionate about fiction as well, particularly with political and economic themes. Dickens, Upton Sinclair, Hall Caine, Victor Hugo, Gorky and Oscar Wilde were among his favourites.'

While in prison, Bhagat Singh and his comrades went on a long hunger strike, raising several demands of the political prisoners. Two of those demands are relevant here:

1. All books, except those proscribed, with writing material, should be made available without restriction.
2. At least one daily paper should be supplied to each political prisoner

Bhagat Singh was almost certain about his martyrdom, yet he wanted to read as much as he could and wanted his comrades to read as well. He could leave behind a huge corpus of written legacy only because his choice of reading material was diverse.

How did he manage to get all this literature, most of which was suspect in the eyes of the colonial administration? There were two main resources for books. One of them was the Dwarka Das Library, established by Lala Lajpat Rai in Lahore and the other was a bookshop called Ramkrishna and Sons. This bookshop had resources to procure banned books from England. Both of them were the main suppliers of Marxist and revolutionary literature. Rajaram Shastri, the young socialist librarian of the library, once told Shiv Verma that Bhagat Singh did not just read books, he almost devoured them, yet his yearning to seek knowledge always remained unsatiated.

Over the years, it has been established that Bhagat Singh was an avid reader. His friend Jaidev Gupta used to supply the specific books he needed in jail. He also recalled that in his late teens, Bhagat Singh 'was always seen with a book in English in his hands and a dictionary in his pocket'. Yashpal, a well-known writer and Bhagat Singh's associate, saw him driving a camel-drawn cart of his father as 'an interesting sight: the camel drove the cart and Bhagat Singh sat in the driver's seat, reading his book'. He also read Bankim's *Anandamath* and Savarkar's book on 1857. Bhagwan Das Mahor recollects that Bhagat Singh had given him a copy of Marx's *Das Kapital*, thereby planting the first seed of socialism in my heart. Unfortunately, this is something not safe or even wise to confess in public today.

Bhagat Singh matured as a political thinker while in prison during the two years he spent there before he was hanged on 23 March 1931. His prison diary clearly reveals the trajectory of his political evolution. It brings into light his reading habits and the wide range of the selection of authors including Marx, Engels, Bertrand Russell, T. Paine, Upton Sinclair, V.I. Lenin, William Wordsworth, Tennyson, Rabindra Nath Tagore, Bukharin, Trotsky, among others. His extensive reading and thinking, while waiting for martyrdom, flowered into one of the most profound essays called 'Why I Am an Atheist'. Bhagat Singh begins the essay by explaining the reasons for writing the piece and it was not vanity, as he was being accused of, that drove him to atheism. 'Some of my friends,' he wrote, 'find it a bit too much on my part to deny the existence of God and that there was a certain amount of vanity that actuated my disbelief.'[5] He went on to say that he is a human being and has all the human traits like anyone else. I had been called an autocrat for imposing my opinion on my friends. He then goes on to stress on ideology when he writes that 'there is vanity in me in as much as our cult as opposed to other popular creeds is concerned. But that is not personal . . .

---

[5] "Why I Am an Atheist", in S. Irfan Habib, op. cit. p. 49.

Vanity or to be more precise "Ahankar" is the excess of undue pride in oneself'. He clarifies strongly that 'it is not this undue pride that has led me to atheism but a serious and careful study of the subject that has led me to the denial of God'.

Bhagat Singh writes about his childhood in the essay, where he says that he was an average student, not liked by some teachers though a favourite with some. He also concedes here that he was a believer as a child, and was brought up chanting Gayatri Mantra. 'I could not get any chance of indulging in such feelings as vanity.' However, he also wants us to know that his 'atheism is not of so recent origin. I had stopped believing in God when I was an obscure young man', though he accepts that at this early stage 'I was not a perfect atheist'.

However, the article had more to it than just the denial of God. It was tinged with a strong rebuttal of blind faith and a zealous defence of reason. Before dealing with his own views about religion, Bhagat Singh first dealt with the religiosity of his predecessors. He points out that in the absence of a scientific understanding of their own political activity, they needed irrational religious beliefs and mysticism to sustain them spiritually, to fight against personal temptation, to overcome depression, to be able to sacrifice their physical comforts, and even life. For this, a person requires deep sources of inspiration. This requirement was, in the case of early revolutionaries, met by mysticism and religion.[6]

He made it clear that the revolutionaries now need no religious inspiration as they have an advanced

---

[6] *The People*, Lahore, 27 September 1931.

revolutionary ideology based on reason instead of blind faith. About God, Bhagat Singh writes:

> He (God) was to serve as a father, mother, sister and brother, friend and helper . . . so that when man be in great distress having been betrayed and deserted by all friends, he may find consolation in the idea that an ever-true friend was still there to help him, to support him and that He was Almighty and could do anything. Really that was useful to a society in the primitive age. The idea of God is helpful to man in distress.[7]

He explains this radical transition in his thinking very succinctly in these words, which he calls a turning point in his life:

> 'Study' was the cry that reverberated in the corridors of my mind. Study to enable yourself to face the arguments advanced by opposition. Study to arm yourself with arguments in favour of your cult. I began to study. My previous faith and convictions underwent a remarkable modification . . . No more mysticism, no more blind faith. Realism became our cult.[8]

Bhagat Singh, in this essay, left behind a scientific world view for all of us to pursue when he says, 'Any man who stands for progress has to criticise, disbelieve and challenge every item of the old faith. Item by item, he has to reason out every nook and corner of the prevailing

---

[7] S. Irfan Habib, op. cit. p. 62–63.

[8] Ibid. p. 52.

faith.' Further, reiterating the strength and worth of reason in human lives, he says that 'his reasoning can be mistaken, wrong, misled and sometimes fallacious. But he is liable to correction because reason is the guiding star of his life. But mere faith and blind faith is dangerous: it dulls the brain and makes a man reactionary'. Bhagat Singh had warned that it is not easy to live the life based on reason while blind faith makes it convenient. Yet, he made a passionate appeal to live the life of reason and be a realist as he did by 'trying to stand like man with an erect head to the last; even on the gallows'.

Bhagat Singh had another interesting discussion in this essay regarding the existence of God and his supposed divine power when he asks all those critics of socialism to request their almighty to enforce equality and also infuse the altruistic enthusiasm in the hearts of all capitalists to forgo their rights of personal possessions . . . and redeem the whole human society. Explaining the imperialist subjugation of India he writes, 'Let me tell you, British rule is here not because God wills it but because they possess power and we do not dare to oppose them. Not that it is with the help of God that they are keeping us under their subjection but it is with the help of guns and rifles . . . and our apathy that they are successfully committing the most deplorable sin against society-the outrageous exploitation of one nation by another.'[9] Bhagat Singh spoke against the ever-prevalent fatalistic belief of the people that humans have no agency while God controls everything.

---

[9] Ibid. p. 61.

While we are wary of teaching evolution and Darwin in schools today[10], Bhagat Singh emphatically wrote about reading Charles Darwin and his *The Origin of Species* to understand the origin of this world and the origin of man. His faith in science, or I must say, his faith in scientific thinking, is palpable throughout the essay. Bhagat Singh also touched upon a very frequently asked question that 'if no God existed, how did the people come to believe in him? My answer is clear and brief. As they came to believe in ghosts, and evil spirits; the only difference is that belief in God is almost universal and the philosophy well developed'.[11] He also hints at the nexus between the exploiters of the people, which included the rich and powerful rulers, holding privileged positions and the belief in God. Bhagat Singh concludes that 'rebellion against king is always a sin according to every religion'.

In a country where the majority of the ideologues of nationalism used one religion or the other to buttress their idea of nationalism, Bhagat Singh as an iconic nationalist showed that religion is not necessarily an imperative for nationalism or for being a nationalist. Thus, most of his quintessential revolutionary nationalism was not underpinned by any religious faith. He was not for a blind flag-waving nationalism, which many of our jingoists need to remember when they revel in his name. His nationalism was embedded in the idea of progress where there is scope for criticism, disbelief and the capacity to

---

[10] https://www.scientificamerican.com/article/india-cuts-periodic-table-and-evolution-from-school-textbooks/

[11] S. Irfan Habib, op. cit. p. 62.

question everything of the old faith. That clearly means that silencing rationalists can't be nationalism. Nor can defending obnoxious religious practices be nationalism. Thus, this essay was not merely a harangue against the very idea of God, it also unconsciously laid down the framework for the youth and strongly conveyed the idea of progressive nationalism.

Bhagat Singh made one more serious comment in the essay where he criticizes all those people who seem to accept the leadership of a leader without questioning or criticism. This is a pertinent comment for our times as well while here Bhagat Singh was referring to the sway of Mahatma Gandhi in the 1920s. He said categorically that if you criticize a great man because he is thought to be infallible, you will be decried as vainglorious. 'Because Mahatmaji is great, therefore none should criticize him. Because he has risen above, therefore everything he says . . . is right. Whether you are convinced or not you must say, "Yes, you are right". This mentality does not lead towards progress. It is rather too obviously, reactionary.'

Besides 'Why I am an Atheist', Bhagat also wrote an insightful introduction to a book of poetry called *The Dreamland* by a senior Ghadar revolutionary L. Ram Saran Das. It is pertinent to see how Das dealt with the problem of conflicting religions; Bhagat Singh observed that the author 'tries to reconcile them (with each other) just as all nationalists try to do', but he was dismissive of the method used and found it lengthy and circuitous. He categorically said: 'On my part, I would have dismissed it with one line by Karl Marx: Religion is the opiate of the masses.' He was convinced that religion was a tool in the hands of exploiters who kept the masses in constant fear of God for their interests. Unfortunately, this comment by Bhagat Singh is reflective of our state of affairs today, where religions have overwhelmed us and polarized the country.

As a thinker and also as a revolutionary, Bhagat Singh was associated with the Hindustan Socialist Republican Association (HSRA), which had realized that all moral ideals and religions were useless for an empty stomach and for him only food was God. Bhagat Singh aptly quoted Horace Greeley in his prison diary saying, 'Morality and religion are but words to him who fishes in gutters for the means of sustaining life, and crouches behind barrels in the street for shelter from the cutting blasts of a winter night'.[12]

This scientific approach of the HSRA leaders matured with the passage of time. The majority of them came close to the ideals of socialism or even communism, which believed in mass action instead of individual acts of terrorism.

We should remember Bhagat Singh with pride and reflect on the alternative framework of governance he had in mind where social and economic justice—and not terrorism or violence—would be supreme. Many of us may not find his commitment to socialism very attractive in these times, yet his concern for the socio-economically deprived sections still commands attention. Moreover, his passionate desire to rise above narrow caste and religious considerations was never as crucial as it is today. It is gratifying to see that a publisher like Penguin India

---

[12] The Jail Notebook of Bhagat Singh

decided to publish 'Why I Am an Atheist' and make it accessible to a larger number of people across the world. After more than four decades of my association with Bhagat Singh's life and thought, it is an honour for me to write an introduction for the essay.

Bhagat Singh was born on 28 September 1907 in a village called Banga in Lyallpur district, now in Pakistan. This village also celebrates his birthday with pride. I am told they commemorate him every year since quite some time, whose birth turned this remote dusty village into a place of pilgrimage. It has been declared as a national heritage site by the Pakistani government. Bhagat Singh evokes respect among many across the border, despite our bitter relationships, because he always advocated for human dignity and rights beyond sectarian divide. He castigated all those who floundered on these basic values, as is evident from this seminal essay called 'Why I Am an Atheist' and also from a fairly huge corpus of writings he bequeathed to us.

S. Irfan Habib
New Delhi
04/05/2024

Know the Revolutionary:
Bhagat Singh

In the early decades of the twentieth century, the fight for India's Independence was at its peak. While leaders like Mahatma Gandhi and Jawaharlal Nehru fought with non-cooperation and non-violence, the revolutionaries gave their sweat and blood to the struggle for independence. Among the many known names was a star that stood out—Bhagat Singh. Laying down his life for the nation at the tender age of twenty-three, he became an idol for many in the years that followed. Celebrated as a young, well-read and meticulous socialist revolutionary, his name is etched in blood in the pages of Indian history as a hero.

Bhagat Singh was born in 1907 in the Punjab Province under British India. His parents, Kishan Singh and Vidyavati, were also a part of the Indian independence movement, so needless to say, Bhagat Singh was exposed to these ideas early on in life. Since his grandfather was a follower of Arya Samaj founded by Swami Dayanand Saraswati, Bhagat Singh was also influenced by it. He also completed his schooling from

DAV High School. When he joined National College in Lahore, he was an all-rounder, studying to his heart's content, and participating in dramatics and essay competitions alongside.

He was deeply influenced by the socialist philosophy, and founded the Indian socialist youth organization, known by the name Naujawan Bharat Sabha in March 1926. He was also a part of the Hindustan Republican Association (HRA), along with Chandrashekhar Azad and Ram Prasad Bismil, among other well-known revolutionary freedom fighters. His family thought he was too deeply involved with the cause of freedom and needed an anchor, and hence thought of arranging his marriage. To escape the same, he ran away. He also gave a firm voice to his thoughts as he edited some Urdu and Punjabi newspapers in Amritsar. His words had the power to transform thoughts, and the British officials ended up arresting him in 1927 for his revolutionary thoughts, seeing him as a potential danger as his ideas were influencing far too many youngsters.

When the Simon Commission visited Lahore in 1928, Lala Lajpat Rai led a march to register protest against the commission. In order to disperse the crowd, the police used lathis, charging Rai in particular. Lala Lajpat Rai died of a heart stroke on 17 November 1928, and as per the doctors, it could have been due to the fatal injuries during the lathi charge.

In a plan to avenge Rai's death, Bhagat Singh, along with Chandrashekhar Azad, Sukhdev Thapar and Shivaram Rajguru planned to kill Scott. But in a case of mistaken identity, they ended up killing a young ASP named J.P. Saunders. The killing was condemned by leaders like Mahatma Gandhi and several leading newspapers too, who stressed on non-cooperation and non-violence. It seemed to have soaked into the public conscience as an act of brave retaliation, making Bhagat Singh a hero.

The four people behind the plan to kill Scott escaped on bicycles to their respective safe houses. They took help from other HSRA members to leave Lahore till the matter was put to rest. Keeping in mind the strong search operation by the police, Bhagat Singh took to western attire, got his hair cut after giving up the turban, donned a hat to cover it, and shaved off his beard.

In the time that followed, Singh continuously worked on inspiring other youngsters to fight for the nation, as against worrying about their life comforts. In one such dramatic act of giving out a message, he proposed to drop bombs in the Central Legislative Assembly. Fighting against the Public Safety Bill and the Trade Disputes Act, they threw pamphlets inside the Legislative Assembly and two bombs inside the corridor. The intent was to warn them, and not cause any loss of life, as Singh and his comrades considered human lives to be of utmost importance. The pamphlet is included in the book and you will find how they clearly mentioned their objective in the same.

Bhagat Singh and Batukeshwar Dutt, who threw the bombs in the Assembly, were arrested and put on trial. Singh was given life imprisonment, but this decision was suspended when the Saunders murder came to light. While on trial, they also went on hunger strikes in the jails they were held in, demanding better facilities for political prisoners. You will also read all those letters in this book.

Bhagat Singh was a well-read man, who knew that their revolution could only be fuelled with the fire of knowledge. His letters to friends will give you an idea of the kind of books he read, and also the ideologies he followed. His famous writing 'Why I Am an Atheist' is a well-articulated opinion of a young man at the threshold of death. Popularizing for the nation and fellow revolutionaries the slogan 'Inquilab Zindabad', he became the flagbearer of the voice of resistance to the British Raj.

While most of the writings included in this book are translated from Punjabi, they will surely give you a peek into the working of a revolutionary mind.

1

Why I Am an Atheist

5 October 1930

Bhagat Singh penned down this essay in Lahore Central Jail in 1930, in response to his religious friends who presumed that he had turned an atheist because of his vanity.

They can kill me, but they cannot kill my ideas.

They can crush my body, but they will not be able to crush my spirit.

— Bhagat Singh

A new question has cropped up. Is it due to vanity that I do not believe in the existence of an omnipotent, omnipresent and omniscient god? I had never imagined that I would ever have to confront such a question. But conversation with some friends has given me a hint that certain of my friends, if I am not claiming too much in thinking them to be so, are inclined to conclude from the brief contact they have had with me, that it was too much on my part to deny the existence of god and that there was a certain amount of vanity that actuated my disbelief. Well, the problem is a serious one. I do not boast to be quite above these human traits. I am a man and nothing more. None can claim to be more. I also have this weakness in me. Vanity does form a part of my nature. Amongst my comrades, I was called an autocrat. Even my friend Mr B.K. Dutt sometimes called me so. On certain occasions, I was decried as a despot. Some friends do complain and very seriously too that I involuntarily thrust my opinions upon others and get my proposals accepted. That this is true up to a certain extent, I do not deny. This may amount to egotism. There is vanity in me in as much as our cult as opposed to other popular creeds is concerned. But that is not personal. It may be, it is only legitimate pride in our cult and does not amount to vanity. Vanity, or to be more precise *"ahankar"*, is the excess of undue pride in one's self. Whether it is such an undue pride that has led me to atheism or whether it is after very careful study of the subject and after much consideration that I have come to disbelieve in god, is a question that I intend to discuss here. Let me first make it clear that egotism and vanity are two different things.

In the first place, I have altogether failed to comprehend as to how undue pride or vain-gloriousness could ever stand in the way of a man in believing in god. I can refuse to recognize the greatness of a really great man provided I have also achieved a certain amount of popularity without deserving it or without having possessed the qualities really essential or indispensable for the same purpose. That much is conceivable. But in what way can a man believing in god cease believing due to his personal vanity? There are only two ways. The man should either begin to think himself a rival of god or he may begin to believe himself to be god. In neither case can he become a genuine atheist. In the first case he does not even deny the existence of his rival. In the second case as well he admits the existence of a conscious being behind the screen, guiding all the movements of nature. It is of no importance to us whether he thinks himself to be that supreme being or whether he thinks the supreme conscious being to be somebody apart from himself. The fundamental is there. His belief is there. He is by no means an atheist. Well, here I am. I neither belong to the first category, nor to the second.

I deny the very existence of that almighty supreme being. Why I deny it shall be dealt with later on. Here, I want to clear one thing, that it is not vanity that has actuated me to adopt the doctrines of atheism. I am neither a rival nor an incarnation nor the supreme being himself. One point is decided, that it is not vanity that has led me to this mode of thinking. Let me examine the facts to disprove this allegation. According to these friends of mine I have grown vain-glorious perhaps due to the undue popularity gained during the trials - both Delhi Bomb and Lahore conspiracy cases. Well, let us see if their premises are correct. My atheism is not of so recent origin. I had stopped believing in god when I was an obscure young man, of whose existence my above mentioned friends were not even aware. At least a college student cannot cherish any short of undue pride which may lead him to atheism. Though a favourite with some professors and disliked by certain others, I was never an industrious or a studious boy. I could not get any chance of indulging in such feelings as vanity. I was rather a boy with a very shy nature, who had certain pessimistic dispositions about the future career. And in those days, I was not a perfect atheist. My grandfather, under whose influence I was brought up, is an orthodox Arya Samajist. An Arya Samajist is anything but an atheist. After finishing my primary education, I joined the DAV School of Lahore and stayed in its boarding house for full one year. There, apart from morning and evening prayers, I used to recite *"Gayatri mantra"* for hours and hours. I was a perfect devotee in those days. Later on, I began to live with my father. He is a liberal in as much as the orthodoxy of religions is concerned. It was through his teachings that I aspired to devote my life to the cause of freedom. But he is not an atheist. He is a firm believer. He used to encourage me for offering prayers daily. So, this is how I was brought up. In the Non-Co operation days, I joined the National College. It was there that I began to think liberally and discuss and criticize all the religious problems, even about god. But still I was a devout believer. By that time I had begun to preserve the unshorn and unclipped long hair, but I could never believe in the mythology and doctrines of Sikhism, or any other religion. But I had a firm faith in god's existence.

Later on I joined the revolutionary party. The first leader with whom I came in contact, though not convinced, could not dare to deny the existence of god. On my persistent inquiries about god, he used to say, "Pray whenever you want to". Now this is atheism less courage required for the adoption of that creed. The second leader with whom I came in contact was a firm believer. Let me mention his name - respected comrade Sachindra Nath Sanyal, now undergoing life transportation in connection with the Karachi conspiracy case. From the very first page of his famous and only book, *Bandi Jivan* (or Incarcerated Life), the glory of god is sung vehemently. In the last page of the second part of that beautiful book his mystic -because of Vedantism - praises showered upon god form a very conspicuous part of his thoughts.

"The Revolutionary leaflet" distributed throughout India on January 28th, 1925 was according to the prosecution story the result of his intellectual labour. Now, as is inevitable in the secret work, the prominent leader expresses his own views, which are very dear to his person and the rest of the workers have to acquiesce in them, in spite of differences which they might have. In that leaflet, one full paragraph was devoted to praise the almighty and his rejoicings and doing. That is all mysticism. What I wanted to point out was that the idea of disbelief had not even germinated in the revolutionary party. The famous Kakori martyrs - all four of them - passed their last day in prayers. Ram Prasad Bismil was an orthodox Arya Samajist. Despite his wide studies in the field of Socialism and Communism, Rajen Lahiri could not suppress his desire of reciting hymns of the Upanishads and the *Gita*. I saw only one man amongst them, who never prayed and used to say, "Philosophy is the outcome of human weakness or limitation of knowledge". He is also undergoing a sentence of transportation for life. But he also never dared to deny the existence of god.

Up to that period, I was only a romantic idealist revolutionary. Uptil then, we were to follow. Now came the time to shoulder the whole responsibility. Due to the inevitable reaction for some time the very existence of the party seemed impossible. Enthusiastic comrades - nay leaders - began to jeer at us. For some time I was afraid that some day I also might not be convinced of the futility of our own program. That was a turning point in my revolutionary career. "Study" was the cry that reverberated in the corridors of my mind. Study to enable yourself to face the arguments advanced by the opposition. Study to arm yourself with arguments in favour of your cult. I began to study. My previous faith and convictions underwent a remarkable modification. The romance of the violent methods alone, which was so prominent amongst our predecessors, was replaced by serious ideas. No more mysticism, no more blind faith. Realism became our cult. Use of force justifiable when resorted to as a matter of terrible necessity, and non-violence as policy indispensable for all mass movements. So much about methods.

The most important thing was the clear conception of the ideal for which we were to fight, As there were no important activities in the field of action, I got ample opportunity to study various ideals of the word revolution. I studied Bakunin, the Anarchist leader; something of Marx, the father of Communism and much of Lenin, Trotsky and others – the men who had successfully carried out a revolution in their country. They were all atheists. Bakunin's "God and State", though only fragmentary, is an interesting study of the subject. Later still I came across a book entitled 'Common Sense' by Nirlamba Swami. It was only a sort of mystic atheism. This subject became of utmost interest to me. By the end of 1926 I had been convinced as to the baselessness of the theory of existence of an almighty supreme being who created, guided and controlled the universe. I had given out this disbelief of mine. I began discussion on the subjects with my friends. I had become a pronounced atheist. But, what it meant will presently be discussed.

In May 1927 I was arrested at Lahore. The arrest was a surprise. I was quite unaware of the fact that the police wanted me. All of a sudden, while passing through a garden, I found myself surrounded by the police. To my own surprise, I was very calm at that time. I did not feel any sensation, neither did I experience any excitement. I was taken into police custody Next day I was taken to the Railway Police lock-up where I was to pass full one month. After many day's conversation with the police officials I guessed that they had some information regarding my connection with the Kakori Party and my other activities in connection with the revolutionary movement. They told me that I had been to Lucknow while the trial was going on there, that I had negotiated a certain scheme about their rescue, that after obtaining their approval, we had procured some bombs, that by way of test one of the bombs was thrown in the crowd on the occasion of Dussehra, 1926. They further informed me, in my interest, that if I could give any statement throwing some light on the activities of the revolutionary party, I was not to be imprisoned but on the contrary set free and rewarded even without being produced as an approver in the court. I laughed at the proposal. It was all humbug.

People holding ideas like ours do not throw bombs on their own innocent people. One fine morning, Mr Newman, the then Senior Superintendent of CID, came to me. And after much sympathetic talk with me imparted to me the extremely sad news that if I did not give any statement as demanded by them, (hey would be forced to send me up for trial for conspiracy to wage war in connection with Kakori case and for brutal murders in connection with Dussehra bomb outrage. And he further informed me that they had evidence enough to get me convicted and hanged.

In those days I believed - though I was quite innocent -the police could do it if they desired. That very day, certain police officials began to persuade me to offer my prayers to god regularly both the times. Now I was an atheist. I wanted to settle for myself whether it was in the days of peace and enjoyment alone that I could boast of being an atheist or whether during such hard times as well I could stick to those principles of mine. After great consideration, I decided that I could not lead myself to believe in and pray to god. No, I never did. That was the real test and I came out successful. Never for a moment did I desire to save my neck at the cost of certain other things. So I was a staunch disbeliever, and have ever since been. It was not an easy job to stand that test.

'Belief' softens the hardships, even can make them pleasant. In god man can find very strong consolation and support. Without Him, man has to depend upon himself. To stand upon one's own legs amid storms and hurricanes is not a child's play. At such testing moments, vanity, if any, evaporates, and man cannot dare to defy the general beliefs. If he does, then we must conclude that he has got certain other strength than mere vanity. This is exactly the situation now. Judgment is already too well known. Within a week, it is to be pronounced. What is the consolation with the exception of the idea that I am going to sacrifice my life for a cause? A god-believing Hindu might be expecting to be reborn as a king, a Muslim or a Christian might dream of the luxuries to be enjoyed in paradise and the reward he is to get for his sufferings and sacrifices. But what am I to expect? I know the moment the rope is fitted round my neck and rafters removed from under my feet, that will be the final moment, that will be the last moment. I, or to be more precise, my soul, as interpreted in the metaphysical terminology, shall all be finished there. Nothing further.

A short life of struggle with no such magnificent end, shall in itself be the reward if I have the courage to take it in that light. That is all. With no selfish motive, or desire to be awarded here or hereafter, quite disinterestedly have I devoted my life to the cause of independence, because I could not do otherwise. The day we find a great number of men and women with this psychology who cannot devote themselves to anything else than the service of mankind and emancipation of the suffering humanity, that day shall inaugurate the era of liberty.

Not to become a king, nor to gain any other rewards here, or in the next birth or after death in paradise, shall they be inspired to challenge the oppressors, exploiters, and tyrants, but to cast off the yoke of serfdom from the neck of humanity and to establish liberty and peace shall they tread this to their individual selves perilous, and to their noble selves the only glorious imaginable - path. Is the pride in their noble cause to be misinterpreted as vanity? Who dares to utter such an abominable epithet? To him, I say either he is a fool or a knave. Let us forgive him for he cannot realize the depth, the emotion, the sentiment and the noble feelings that surge in that heart. His heart is dead as a mere lump of flesh, his eyes are weak, the evils of other interests having been cast over them. Self-reliance is always liable to be interpreted as vanity. It is sad and miserable but there is no help.

You go and oppose the prevailing faith, you go and criticize a hero, a great man, who is generally believed to be above criticism because he is thought to be infallible, the strength of your argument shall force the multitude to decry you as vainglorious. This is due to the mental stagnation. Criticism and independent thinking are the two indispensable qualities of a revolutionary. Because Mahatamaji is great, therefore none should criticize him. Because he has risen above, therefore everything he says- may be in the field of politics or religion, economics or ethics- is right. Whether you are convinced or not, you must say, "Yes, that's true". This mentality does not lead towards progress. It is rather too obviously reactionary.

Because our forefathers had set up a faith in some supreme, being - the Almighty God - therefore any man who dares to challenge the validity of that faith, or the very existence of that supreme being, he shall have to be called an apostate, a renegade. If his arguments are too sound to be refuted by counterarguments and spirit too strong to be cowed down by the threat of misfortunes that may befall him by the wrath of the almighty he shall be decried as vainglorious, his spirit to be denominated as vanity. Then why to waste time in this vain discussion? Why try to argue out the whole thing? This question is coming before the public for the first time, and is being handled in this matter of fact way for the first time, hence this lengthy discussion.

As for the first question, I think I have cleared that it is not vanity that has led me to atheism. My way of argument has proved to be convincing or not, that is to be judged by my readers, not me. I know in the present circumstances, my faith in god would have made my life easier, my burden lighter and my disbelief in him has turned all the circumstances too dry and the situation may assume too harsh a shape. A little bit of mysticism can make it poetical. But I do not want the help of any intoxication to meet my fate. I am a realist. I have been trying to overpower the instinct in me by the help of reason. I have not always been successful in achieving this end. But man's duty is to try and endeavour, success depends upon chance and environments.

As for the second question that if it was not vanity, then there ought to be some reason to disbelieve the old and still prevailing faith of the existence of god. Yes, I come to that now. Reason there is. According to me, any man who has got some reasoning power at his command always tries to reason out his environments. Where direct proofs are lacking, philosophy occupies the important place. As I have already stated, a certain revolutionary friend used to say that philosophy is the outcome of human weakness. When our ancestors had leisure enough to try to solve out the mystery of this world, its past, present and the future, its whys and wherefores, they having been terribly short of direct proofs, everybody tried to solve the problem in his own way. Hence we find the wide differences in the fundamentals of various religious creeds, which sometimes assume very antagonistic and conflicting shapes. Not only the Oriental and Occidental philosophies differ, there are differences even amongst various schools of thoughts in each hemisphere. Amongst Oriental religions, the Moslem faith is not at all compatible with Hindu faith. In India alone, Buddhism and Jainism are sometimes quite separate from Brahmanism, in which there are again conflicting faiths as Arya Samaj and Sanatan Dharma. Charwak is still another independent thinker of the past ages. He challenged the authority of god in the old times. All these creeds differ from each other on the fundamental question, and everybody considers himself to be on the right. There lies the misfortune. Instead of using the experiments and expressions of the ancient savants and thinkers as a basis for our future struggle against ignorance, and to try to find out a solution to this mysterious problem, we - lethargical as we have proved to be - raise the hue and cry of faith, unflinching and unwavering faith to their versions, and thus, are guilty of stagnation in human progress.

Any man who stands for progress has to criticize, disbelieve and challenge every item of the old faith. Item by item he has to reason out every nook and corner of the prevailing faith. If after considerable reasoning one is led to believe in any theory or philosophy, his faith is welcomed. His reasoning can be mistaken, wrong, misled and sometimes fallacious. But he is liable to correction because reason is the guiding star of his life. But mere faith and blind faith is dangerous; it dulls the brain, and makes a man reactionary.

A man who claims to be a realist has to challenge the whole of the ancient faith. If it does not stand the onslaught of reason, it crumbles down. Then the first thing for him is to shatter the whole down and clear a space for the erection of a new philosophy. This is the negative side. After it begins the positive work, in which sometimes some material of the old faith may be used for the purpose of reconstruction. As far as I am concerned, let me admit at the very outset that I have not been able to study much on this point. I had a great desire to study the Oriental Philosophy, but I could not get any chance or opportunity to do the same. But so far as the negative study is under discussion, I think I am convinced to the extent of questioning the soundness of the old faith. I have been convinced as to the non-existence of a conscious supreme being who is guiding and directing the movements of nature. We believe in nature and the whole progressive movement aims at the domination of man over nature for his service. There is no conscious power behind it to direct. This is what our philosophy is.

As for the negative side, we ask a few questions from the 'believers'.

If, as you believe, there is an almighty, omnipresent, omniscient and omnipotent god - who created the earth or world - please let me know why did he create it? This world of woes and miseries, a veritable, eternal combination of numberless tragedies: Not a single soul being perfectly satisfied.

Pray, don't say that it is His Law. If he is bound by any law, he is not omnipotent. He is another slave like ourselves. Please don't say that it is his enjoyment. Nero burnt one Rome. He killed a very limited number of people. He created very few tragedies, all to his perfect enjoyment. And what is his place in history? By what names do the historians mention him? All the venomous epithets are showered upon him. Pages are blackened with invective diatribes condemning Nero, the tyrant, the heartless, the wicked.

One Changez Khan sacrificed a few thousand lives to seek pleasure in it and we hate the very name. Then how are you going to justify your almighty, eternal Nero, who has been, and Is still causing numberless tragedies every day, every[7] hour and every minute? How do you think to support his misdoings which surpass those of Changez every single moment? I say why did he create this world - a veritable hell, a place of constant and bitter unrest? Why did the almighty create man when he had the power not to do it? What is the justification for all this ? Do you say to award the innocent sufferers hereafter and to punish the wrong-doers as well? Well, well... How far shall you justify a man who may dare to inflict wounds upon your body to apply a very soft and soothing liniment upon it afterwards? How far the supporters and organizers of the Gladiator Institution were justified in throwing men before the half-starved furious lions to be cared for and well looked after if they could survive and manage to escape death by the wild beasts? That is why I ask, 'Why did the conscious supreme being create this world and man in it? To seek pleasure? Where then is the difference between him and Nero?'

You Mohammadens and Christians: Hindu philosophy shall still linger on to offer another argument. I ask you, what is your answer to the above-mentioned question? You don't believe in previous birth. Like Hindus, you cannot advance the argument of previous misdoings of the apparently quite innocent sufferers. I ask you why did the omnipotent labour for six days to create the world through word and each day to say that all was well. Call him today. Show him the past history. Make him study the present situation. Let us see if he dares to say "All is well".

From the dungeons of prisons, from the stores of starvation consuming millions upon millions of human beings in slums and huts, from the exploited labourers, patiently or say apathetically watching the procedure of their blood being sucked by the Capitalist vampires, and the wastage of human energy that will make a man with the least common sense shiver with horror, and from the preference of throwing the surplus of production in oceans rather than to distribute amongst the needy producers... to the palaces of kings built upon the foundation laid with human bones... let him see all this and let him say "All is well".

Why and wherefore? That is my question. You are silent.

All right then, I proceed. Well, you Hindus, you say all the present sufferers belong to the class of sinners of the previous births. Good. You say the present oppressors were saintly people in their previous births, hence they enjoy power. Let me admit that your ancestors were very shrewd people, they tried to find out theories strong enough to hammer down all the efforts of reason and disbelief. But let us analyze how far this argument can really stand.

From the point of view of the most famous jurists, punishment can be justified only from three or four ends to meet which it is inflicted upon the wrongdoer. They are retributive, reformative and deterrent. The retributive theory is now being condemned by all the advanced thinkers. Deterrent theory is also following the same fate. Reformative theory is the only one which is essential, and indispensable for human progress. It aims at returning the offender as a most competent and a peace-loving citizen to the society. But what is the nature of punishment inflicted by god upon men, even if we suppose them to be offenders? You say he sends them to be born as a cow, a cat, a tree, a herb or a beast. You enumerate these punishments to be eighty-four lakhs. I ask you, what is its reformative effect upon man? How many men have met you who say that they were born as a donkey In previous birth for having committed any sin? None. Don't quote your Puranas. I have no scope to touch your mythologies. Moreover, do you know that the greatest sin in this world is to be poor. Poverty is a sin; it is a punishment.

I ask you how far would you appreciate a criminologist, a jurist or a legislator who proposes such measures of punishment which shall inevitably force man to commit more offences? Had not your god thought of this or he also had to learn these things by experience, but at the cost of untold sufferings to be borne by humanity? What do you think shall be the fate of a man who has been born in a poor and illiterate family of say a chamar or a sweeper. He is poor, hence he cannot study. He is hated and shunned by his fellow human beings who think themselves to be his superiors, having been born in a higher caste. His ignorance, his poverty and the treatment meted out to him shall harden his heart towards society. Suppose he commits a sin, who shall bear the consequences? God, he or the learned ones of the society? What about the punishment of those people who were deliberately kept ignorant by the haughty and egotist Brahmans and who had to pay the penalty by bearing the stream of being led (not lead) in their ears for having heard a few sentences of your sacred books of learning - the Vedas? If they committed any offence, who was to be responsible for them and who was to bear the brunt? My dear friends, these theories are the inventions of the privileged ones. They justify their usurped power, riches and superiority by the help of these theories. Yes, it was perhaps Upton Sinclair that wrote at some place, that just make a man a believer in immortality and then rob him of all his riches and possessions. He shall help you even in that ungrudgingly. The coalition amongst the religious preachers and possessors of power brought forth jails, gallows, knouts and these theories.

I ask why your omnipotent god, does not stop every man when he is committing any sin or offence? He can do it quite easily Why did he not kill war lords or kill the fury of war in them and thus avoid the catastrophe hurled down on the head of humanity by the Great War?

Why does he not just produce a certain sentiment in the mind of the British people to liberate India? Why does he not infuse the altruistic enthusiasm in the hearts of all capitalists to forgo their rights of personal possessions of means of production and thus redeem the whole labouring community - nay, the whole human society from the bondage of Capitalism. You want to reason out the practicability of socialist theory, I leave it for your almighty to enforce it.

People recognize the merits of socialism in as much as the general welfare is concerned. They oppose it under the pretext of its being impracticable. Let the almighty step in and arrange everything in an orderly fashion. Now don't try to advance round about arguments; they are out of order. Let me tell you, British rule is here not because god wills it, but because they possess power and we do not dare to oppose them. Not that it is with the help of god that they are keeping us under their subjection, but It is with the help of guns and rifles, bomb and bullets, police and millitia and our apathy that they are successfully committing the most deplorable sin against society - the outrageous exploitation of one nation by another. Where is god? What is he doing? Is he enjoying all these woes of human race? A Nero; a Changez. Down with him!

Do you ask me how I explain the origin of this world and origin of man? Alright, I will tell you. Charles Darwin has tried to throw some light on the subject. Study him. Read Soham Swamis "Commonsense". It shall answer your question to some extent. This is a phenomenon of nature. The accidental mixture of different substances in the shape of nebulae produced this earth. When? Consult history The same process produced animals and in the long run, man. Read Darwins *Origin of Species.* And all the later progress is due to man's constant conflict with nature and his efforts to override it. This is the briefest possible explanation of this phenomenon.

Your other argument may be just to ask why a child is born blind or lame, if not due to his deeds committed in the previous birth? This problem has been explained away by biologists as a more biological phenomenon. According to them, the whole burden rests upon the shoulders of the parents, who may be conscious or ignorant of their own deeds that led to mutilation of the child previous to its birth.

Naturally, you may ask another question, though it is quite childish in essence. If no god existed, how did the people come to believe in him? My answer is clear and brief. As they came to believe in ghosts and evil spirits; the only difference is that belief in god is almost universal and the philosophy well developed. Unlike certain of the radicals, I would not attribute its origin to the ingenuity of the exploiters who wanted to keep the people under their subjection by preaching the existence of a supreme being and then claiming an authority and sanction from him for their privileged positions. Though I do not differ with them on the essential point that all faiths, religions, creeds and such other institutions became in turn the mere supporters of the tyrannical and exploiting institutions, men and classes. Rebellion against king is always a sin according to every religion.

As regards the origin of god, my own idea is that having realized the limitations of man, his weaknesses and shortcoming having been taken into consideration, god was brought into imaginary existence to encourage man to face boldly all the trying circumstances, to meet all dangers manfully and to check and restrain his outbursts in prosperity and affluence. God, both with his private laws and parental generosity, was imagined and painted in greater details. He was to serve as a deterrent factor when his fury and private laws were discussed so that man may not become a danger to society. He was to serve as a father, mother, sister and brother, friend and helpers when his parental qualifications were to be explained. So that when man be in great distress, having been betrayed and deserted by all friends, he may find consolation in the idea that an ever true friend was still there to help him, to support him and that he was almighty and could do anything. Really, that was useful to the society in the primitive age.

The idea of god is helpful to a man in distress.

Society has to fight out this belief as well as idol worship and the narrow conception of religion. Similarly, when man tries to stand on his own legs, and become a realist he shall have to throw the faith aside, and to face manfully all the distress, trouble in which the circumstances may throw him. That is exactly my state of affairs. It is not my vanity, my friends. It is my mode of thinking that has made me an atheist. I don't know whether in my case belief in god and offering of daily prayers - which I consider to be most selfish and degraded act on the part of man can prove to be helpful or they shall make my case worse still. I have read of atheists facing all troubles quite boldly, so am I trying to stand like a man with an erect head to the last; even on the gallows.

Let us see how I carry on. One friend asked me to pray. When informed of my atheism, he said, "During your last days you will begin to believe." I said, "No, dear sir, it shall not be. I will think that to be an act of degradation and demoralization on my part. For selfish motives, I am not going to pray. Readers and friends, "Is this vanity"? If it is, I stand for it.

2

I Would Not Defend Myself

4 October 1930

Bhagat Singh wrote this letter to his father Sardar Kishan Singh when he found out that the latter was trying to prove him innocent in the case of Sounder's death. His father had made a written request to the Tribunal of Lahore Conspiracy case stating that Bhagat Singh be given a chance to prove his innocence.

"The sword of revolution is sharpened on the whetting stone of ideas."

- Bhagat Singh

My Dear Father,

I was astounded to learn that you had submitted a petition to the members of the Special Tribunal in connection with my defence. This intelligence proved to be too severe a blow to be borne with equanimity. It has upset the whole equilibrium of my mind. I have not been able to understand how you could think it proper to submit such a petition at this stage and in these circumstances. Inspite of all the sentiments and feelings of a father, I don't think you were at all entitled to make such a move on my behalf without even consulting me. You know that in the political field, my views have always differed with those of yours. I have always been acting independently without having cared for your approval or disapproval.

I hope you can recall to yourself that since the very beginning, you have been trying to convince me to fight my case very seriously and to defend myself properly. But you also know that I was always opposed to it. I never had any desire to defend myself and never did I seriously think about it. Whether it was a mere vague ideology or that I had certain arguments to justify my position, is a different question and that cannot be discussed here.

You know that we have been pursuing a definite policy in this trial. Every action of mine ought to have been consistent with that policy, my principle and my programme, At present the circumstances are altogether different, but had the situation been otherwise, even then I would have been the last man to offer defence. I had only one idea before me throughout the trial, i.e. In show complete indifference towards the trial, in spite of the serious nature of the charges against us. I have always been of the opinion that all the political workers should be indifferent and should never bother about the legal fight in the law courts, and should boldly bear the heaviest possible sentences inflicted upon them. They may defend themselves, but always from purely political considerations and never from a personal point of view. Our policy in this trial has always been consistent with this principle; whether we were successful in that or not is not for me to judge. We have always been doing our duty quite disinterstedly.

In the statement accompanying the text of Lahore Conspiracy Case Ordinance, the Viceroy had stated that the accused in this case were trying to bring both law and justice into contempt. The situation afforded us an opportunity to show to the public whether we were trying to bring law into contempt or whether others were doing so. People might disagree with us on this point. You might be one of them. But that never meant that such moves should be made on my behalf without my consent or even my knowledge. My life is not so precious, at least to me, as you may probably think it to be. It is not at all worth buying at the cost of my principles. There are other comrades of mine whose case is as serious as that of mine. We had adopted a common policy and we shall stand to the last, no matter how dearly we have to pay individually for it.

Father, I am quite perplexed. I fear I might overlook the ordinary principle of etiquette and my language may become a little bit harsh while criticizing or rather censoring this move on your part. Let me be candid. I feel as though I have been stabbed in the back. Had any other person done it, I would have considered it to be nothing short of treachery. But in your case, let me say that it has been a weakness - a weakness of the worst type.

This was the time where everybody's mettle was being tested. Let me say, father, you have failed. I know you are as sincere a patriot as one can be. I know you have devoted your life to the cause of Indian independence, but why, at this moment, have you displayed such a weakness? I cannot understand.

In the end, I would like to inform you and my other friends and all the people interested in my case, that I have not approved of your move. I am still not at all in favour of offering any defence. Even if the court had accepted that petition submitted by some of my co-accused regarding defence, etc., I would have not defended myself. My applications submitted to the Tribunal regarding my interview during the hunger strike were misinterpreted and it was published in the press that I was going to offer defence, though in reality I was never willing to offer any defence. I still hold the same opinion as before. My friends in the Borstal Jail will be taking it as a treachery and betrayal on my part. I shall not even get an opportunity to clear my position before them.

I want that public should know all the details about this complication, and therefore, I request you to publish this letter.

Your loving son,
Bhagat Singh

3

Letter To Shaheed Sukhdev

5 April 1929

*Written by Bhagat Singh in Sita Ram Bazar in Delhi
this letter was delivered to Sukhdev in Lahore by Shiv
Verma, only to be recovered from him at the time of his
arrest a week later.*

"Revolution is an inalienable right of mankind. Freedom is an imperishable birthright of all."

- Bhagat Singh

Dear Brother,

By the time you receive this letter, I will be gone, going to a far off destination. Let me assure that I am prepared for the voyage in spite of all the sweet memories and in spite of all the charms of my life here. Up to this day, one thing pinched in my heart and it was this - that my brother, my own brother, misunderstood and accused me of a very serious charge -the charge of weakness. Today I am quite satisfied, today more than ever do I feel that was nothing, but a misunderstanding, a wrong calculation. My over-frankness was interpreted as my talkativeness, and my confession as my weakness. And now I feel it was misunderstanding and only misunderstanding. I am not weak, not weaker than anyone amongst us, brother. With a clear heart I go. Will you clear too? It will be very kind of you. Hut note that you are to take no hasty step, soberly and calmly you are to carry on the work. Don't try to take the chance at the very outset. You have some duty towards the public, and that you can fulfill by continuing this work. As a suggestion, I would say that M.R. Shastri appeals to me more than ever. Try to bring him into the arena, provided he himself may be willing, clearly knowing the dark future. Let him mix with men and study their psychology. If he will work in the right spirit, he will be the better judge. Arrange as you may deem fit. Now, brother, let us be happy.

By the way, I must say that I cannot help arguing once again my case in the matter under discussion. Again do I emphasise that I am full of ambition and hope and of full charm of life. But I can renounce all at the time of need, and that is the real sacrifice. These things can never be hinderance in the way of man, provided he be a man. You will have the practical proof in the near future. While discussing anybody's character, you asked me one thing, whether love ever proved helpful to any man. Yes, I answer that question today. To Mazzini, it was. You must have read that after the utter failure and crushing defeat of his first rising, he could not bear the misery and haunting ideas of his dead comrades. He would have gone mad or committed suicide but for one letter of a girl he loved. He would feel as strong as anyone, nay stronger than all. As regards the moral status of love, I may say that it in itself is nothing but passion; not an animal passion, but a human one, and very sweet too. Love in itself can never be an animal passion. Love always elevates the character of man. It never lowers him, provided love be love. You can't call these girls - mad people, as we generally see in films - lovers. They always play in the hands of animal passions. The true love cannot be created. It comes of its own accord, nobody can say when. It is but natural. And I may tell you that a young man and a young girl can love each other, and with the aid of their love they can overcome the passions themselves and can maintain their purity. I may clear one thing here; when I said that love has human weakness, I did not say it for an ordinary human being at this stage, where the people generally are. But that is the most idealistic stage when man would overcome all these sentiments, the love, the hatred, and so on. When man will lake reason as the sole basis of his activity. But at present, it is not bad, rather good and useful to man. And moreover, while rebuking the love, I rebuked the love of one individual for one, and that too in idealistic stage. And even then, man must have the strongest feelings of love which he may not confine to one individual and may make it universal. Now I think I have cleared my position. One thing I may tell you to mark; we in spite of all radical ideas that we cherish, have not been able to do away with the overidealistic Arya Samajist conception of morality We may talk glibly about all the radical things that can possibly be conceived, but in practical life, we begin to tremble at the very outset. This I will request you do away with. And may I, without fear at all the misapprehension in my mind, request you do kindly lower the standard of your over-idealism a bit, not to be harsh to those who will live behind and will be the victims of a disease as myself ? Don't rebuke them and thus add to their woes and miseries. They need your sympathy. May I repeat that you, without bearing any sort of grudge against any particular individual, will sympathise with those who need it the most? But you cannot realise these things unless and until you yourself fall a victim to this. But, why I am writing all this? I wanted to be frank. I have cleared my heart.

Wish you all success and happy life.

Yours,
B.S.

4

The Red Pamphlet

8 April 1929

This leaflet was left all across the Central Assembly Hall by Bhagat Singh and Batukeshwar Dutt after they threw two bombs in the assembly corridor.

"Old orders should change, always and ever, yielding place to new, so that one good order may not corrupt the world."

– Bhagat Singh

The Hindustan Socialist Republican Army (Notice)

It takes a loud voice to make the deaf hear, with these immortal words uttered on a similar occasion by Valiant, a French anarchist martyr, do we strongly justify this action of ours.

Without repeating the humiliating history of the past ten years of the working of the reforms (Montague-Chelmsford Reforms) and without mentioning the insults hurled at the Indian nation through this House - the so-called Indian Parliament - we want to point out that, while the people expecting some more crumbs of reforms from the Simon Commission, and are ever quarrelling over the distribution of the expected bones, the government is thrusting upon us new repressive measures like the Public Safety and the Trade Disputes Bill, while reserving the Press Sedition Bill for the next session. The indiscriminate arrests of labour leaders working in the open field clearly indicate whither the wind blows.

In these extremely provocative circumstances, the Hindustan Socialist Republican Association, in all seriousness, realizing their full responsibility, had decided and ordered its army to do this particular action, so that a stop be put to this humiliating farce and to let the alien bureaucratic exploiters do what they wish, but they must be made to come before the public, even in their naked form.

Let the representatives of the people return to their constituencies and prepare the masses for the coming revolution, and let the government know that while protesting against the Public Safety and Trade Disputes Bills and the callous murder of Lala Lajpat Rai, on behalf of the helpless Indian masses, we want to emphasize the lesson often repeated by history, that it is easy to kill individuals, but you cannot kill the ideas. Great empires crumbled while the ideas survived, Bourbons and Czars fell, while the revolution marched ahead triumphantly.

We are sorry to admit that we, who attach so great a sanctity to human life, who dream of a glorious future, when man will be enjoying perfect peace and full liberty, have been forced to shed human blood. But the sacrifice of individuals at the altar of the 'Great Revolution' that will bring freedom to all, rendering the exploitation of man by man impossible, is inevitable.

"Long live the revolution."

Signed,
Balraj
Commander-in-Chief

5

Statement of Bhagat Singh and B.K Dutt in the Assembly Bomb Case

6 June 1929

This is a copy of the statement made by Bhagat Singh and Batukeshwar Dutt after they threw bombs in the Central Assembly Hall and were arrested for the same.

We stand charged with certain serious offences, and at this stage, it is but right that we must explain our conduct. In this connection, the following questions arise.

1. Were the bombs thrown into the Chamber. And, if so, why?
2. Is the charge, as framed by the Lower Court, correct or otherwise?

To the first half of the first question, our reply is in the affirmative, but since some of the so-called 'eye witnesses' have perjured themselves and since we are not denying our liability to that extent, let our statement about them be judged for what it is worth. By way of an illustration, we may point out that the evidence of Sergeant Terry regarding the seizure of the pistol from one of us is a deliberate falsehood, for neither of us had the pistol at the time we gave ourselves up. Other witnesses, too, who have deposed to having seen bombs being thrown by us have not scrupled to tell lies. This fact had its own moral for those who aim at judicial purity and fair play. At the same time, we acknowledge the fairness of the Public Prosecutor and the judicial attitude of the Court so far.

Viceroy's Views Endorsed

In our reply to the next half of the first question, we are constrained to go into some detail to offer a full and frank explanation of our motive and the circumstances leading up to what has now become a historic event.

When we were told by some of the police officers, who visited us in jail, that Lord Irwin in his address to the joint session of the two houses described the event as an attack directed against no individual but against an institution itself, we readily recognized that the true significance of the incident had been correctly appreciated. We are next to none in our love for humanity. Far from having any malice against any individual, we hold human life sacred beyond words. We are neither perpetrators of dastardly outrages, and, therefore, a disgrace to the country -as the pseudo-socialist Dewan Chaman Lal is reported to have described us; nor are we lunatics' as *The Tribune* of Lahore and some others would have it believed.

Practical Protest

We humbly claim to be no more than serious students of the history and conditions of our country and her aspirations. We despise hypocrisy. Our practical protest was against the institution, which since its birth, has eminently helped to display not only its worthlessness, but its far-reaching power for mischief. The more we have been convinced that it exists only to demonstrate to world Indian's humiliation and helplessness, and it symbolizes the overriding domination of an irresponsible and autocratic rule. Time and again, the national demand has been pressed by the peoples representatives only to find the waste paper basket as its final destination.

Attack on Institution

Solemn resolutions passed by the House have been contemptuously trampled under foot on the floor of the

so-called Indian Parliament. Resolution regarding the
repeal of the repressive and arbitrary measures have been
treated with sublime contempt, and the government
measures and proposals, rejected as unacceptable by the
elected members of the legislatures, have been restored
by mere stroke of the pen. In short, we have utterly failed
to find any justification for the existence of an institution
which, despite all its pomp and splendour, organized with
the hard earned money of the sweating millions of India,
is only a hollow show and a mischievous make-believe.
Alike, have we failed to comprehend the mentality of
the public leaders who help the government to squander
public time and money on such a manifestly stage-
managed exhibition of Indian's helpless subjection.

No Hope For Labour

We have been ruminating upon all these matters, as
also upon the wholesale arrests of the leaders of the
labour movement. When the introduction of the Trade
Disputes Bill brought us into the Assembly to watch its
progress, the course of the debate only served to confirm
our conviction that the labouring millions of India had
nothing to expect from an institution that stood as a
menacing monument to the strangling of the exploiters
and the serfdom of the helpless labourers.

Finally, the insult of what we consider an inhuman and
barbarous measure was hurled on the devoted head of
the representatives of the entire country, and the starving
and struggling millions were deprived of their primary
right and the sole means of improving their economic
welfare. None who has felt like us for the dumb driven
drudges of labourers could possibly witness this spectacle

with equanimity None whose heart bleeds for them, who have given their life-blood in silence to the building up of the economic structure could repress the cry which this ruthless blow had wrung out of our hearts.

Bomb Needed

Consequently, bearing in mind the words of the late Mr. S.R. Das, once Law Member of the Governor - Generals Executive Council, which appeared in the famous letter he had addressed to his son, to the effect that the 'Bomb was necessary to awaken England from her dreams', we dropped the bomb on the floor of the Assembly Chamber to register our protest on behalf of those who had no other means left to give expression to their heartrending agony. Our sole purpose was "to make the deaf hear" and to give the heedless a timely warning. Others have as keenly felt as we have done, and from under the seeming stillness of the sea of Indian humanity, a veritable storm is about to break out. We have only hoisted the "danger-signal" to warn those who are speeding along without heeding the grave dangers ahead. We have only marked the end of an era of Utopian non-violence, of whose futility the rising generation has been convinced beyond the shadow of doubt.

Ideal Explained

We have used the expression Utopian non-violence in the foregoing paragraph which requires some explanation. Force when aggressively applied is "violence" and is, therefore, morally unjustifiable, but when it is used in the furtherance of a legitimate cause, it has its moral justification. The elimination of force at all costs in

Utopian, and the new movement which has arisen in the country, and of that dawn we have given a warning, is inspired by the ideal which guided Guru Gobind Singh and Shivaji, Kamal Pasha and Riza Khan, Washington and Garibaldi, Lafayette and Lenin.

As both the alien government and the Indian public leaders appeared to have shut their eyes to the existence of this movement, we felt it as our duty to sound a warning where it could not go unheard. We have so far dealt with the motive behind the incident in question, and now we must define the extent of our intention.

No Personal Grudge

We bore no personal grudge or malice against anyone of those who received slight injuries or against any other person in the Assembly. On the contrary, we repeat that we hold human life sacred beyond words, and would sooner lay down our own lives in the service of humanity than injure anyone else. Unlike the mercenary soldiers of the imperialist armies who are disciplined to kill without compunction, we respect, and, in so far as it lies in our power, we attempt to save human life. And still we admit having deliberately thrown the bombs into the Assembly Chamber. Facts, however, speak for themselves and our intention would be judged from the result of the action without bringing in Utopian hypothetical circumstances and presumptions.

No Miracle

Despite the evidence of the government expert, the bombs that were thrown in the Assembly Chamber resulted in slight damage to an empty bench and some slight abrasions in less than half a dozen cases, while government scientists and experts have ascribed this result to a miracle, we see nothing but a precisely scientific process in all this incident. Firstly, the two bombs exploded in vacant spaces within the wooden barriers of the desks and benches; secondly, even those who were within 2 feet of the explosion, for instance, Mr. P. Ran, Mr. Shanker Rao and Sir George Schuster were either not hurt or only slightly scratched. Bombs of the capacity deposed to by the government expert (though his estimate being imaginary is exaggerated), loaded with an effective charge of potassium chlorate and sensitive (explosive) picrate would have smashed the barriers and laid many low within some yards of the explosion.

Again, had they been loaded with some other high explosive, with a charge of destructive pellets or darts, they would have sufficed to wipe out a majority of the members of the Legislative Assembly. Still again we could have flung them into the official box which was occupied by some notable persons. And finally we could have ambushed Sir John Simon whose luckless commission was loathed by all responsible people and who was sitting in the President's gallery at the time. All these things, however, were beyond our intention and bombs did no more than they were designed to do, and the miracle consisted in no more than the deliberate aim which landed them in safe places.

We then deliberately offered ourselves to bear the penalty for what we had done and to let the imperialist exploiters know that by crushing individuals, they cannot kill ideas. By crushing two insignificant units, a nation cannot be crushed. We wanted to emphasize the historical lesson that lettres de cachets and Bastilles could not crush the revolutionary movement in France. Gallows

and the Siberian mines could not extinguish the Russian
Revolution. Bloody Sunday, and Black and Tans failed to
strangle the movement of Irish freedom. Can ordinances
and safety bills snuff out the flames of freedom in India?
Conspiracy cases, trumped up or discovered, and the
incarceration of all young men, who cherish the vision of
a great ideal, cannot check the march of revolution. But a
timely warning, if not unheeded, can help to prevent loss
of life and general sufferings. We took it upon ourselves
to provide this warning and our duty is done.

"Revolution" does not necessarily involve sanguinary
strife, nor is there any place in it for individual vendetta. It
is not the cult of the bomb and the pistol. By "Revolution"
we mean that the present order of things, which is based
on manifest injustice, must change. Producers or labourers
in spite of being the most necessary element of society,
are robbed by their exploiters of the fruits of their labour
and deprived of their elementary rights. The peasant who
grows corn for all, starves with his family; the weaver who
supplies the world market with textile fabrics, has not
enough to cover his own and his children's bodies; masons,
smiths and carpenters who raise magnificent palaces, live
like pariahs in the slums. The capitalists and exploiters,
the parasites of society, squander millions on their whims.
These terrible inequalities and forced disparity of chances
are bound to lead to chaos. This state of affairs cannot last
long, and it is obvious, that the present order of society in
merry-making is on the brink of a volcano.

The whole edifice of this civilization, if not saved
in time, shall crumble. A radical change, therefore, is
necessary and it is the duty of those who realize it to
reorganize society on the socialistic basis. Unless this

thing is done and the exploitation of man by man and of nations by nations is brought to an end, sufferings and carnage with which humanity is threatened today cannot be prevented. All talk of ending war and ushering in an era of universal peace is undisguised hypocrisy.

By "Revolution", we mean the ultimate establishment of an order of society which may not be threatened by such breakdown, and in which the sovereignty of the proletariat should be recognized and a world federation should redeem humanity from the bondage of capitalism and misery of imperial wars.

This is our ideal, and with this ideology as our inspiration; we have given a fair and loud enough warning.

If, however, it goes unheeded and the present system of government continues to be an impediment in the way of the natural forces that are swelling up, a grim struggle will ensure, involving the overthrow of all obstacles, and the establishment of the dictatorship of the proletariat to pave the way for the consummation of the ideal of revolution. Revolution is an inalienable right of mankind. Freedom is an imperishable birth right of all. Labour is the real sustainer of society. The sovereignty of the ultimate destiny of the workers.

For these ideals, and for this faith, we shall welcome any suffering to which we may be condemned. At the altar of this revolution we have brought our youth as an incense, for no sacrifice is too great for so magnificent a cause. We are content, we await the advent of revolution.

"Long live the revolution."

6

Demands for Political Prisoners

24 June 1929

Bhagat Singh and B.K. Dutt were sentenced to transportation for life (an alternative sentence to hanging, wherein the convicts were moved to jails in colonies to serve their sentence) in Mianwali and Lahore jails, respectively. They held hunger strikes at their respective prisons to ensure better treatment for political prisoners. Subsequently, Bhagat Singh was also sent to the Lahore jail, where the two carried on the crusade and wrote the following letter to the Home Member in Government of India to list their demands.

Central Jail
Lahore
24.6.29

We, Bhagat Singh and B.K. Dutt, were sentenced to life transportation in the Assembly Bomb Case, Delhi on the 19th April, 1929. As long as we were under trial prisoners in Delhi jail, we were accorded a very good treatment from that jail to the Mianwali and Lahore Central jails, respectively. We wrote an application to the higher authorities asking for better diet and a few other facilities, and refused to take the jail diet.

Our demands were as follows:

We, as political prisoners, should be given a better diet and the standard of our diet should at least be the same as that of European prisoners. (It is not the sameness of dietary that we demand, but the sameness of standard of diet.)

We shall not be forced to do any hard and undignified lobours at all.

All books, other than those proscribed, along with writing materials, should be allowed to us without any restriction.

At least one standard daily paper should be supplied to every political prisoner.

Political prisoners should have a special ward of their own in every jail, provided with all necessities as those of the Europeans. And all the political prisoners in one jail must be kept together in that ward.

Toilet necessities should be supplied.

Better clothing.

We have explained above the demands that we made. They are the most reasonable demands. Jail authorities told us one day that the higher authorities have refused to comply with our demands.

Apart from that, they handle us very roughly while feeding us artificially, and Bhagat Singh was lying quite senseless on the 10th June, 1929, for about fifteen minutes, after the forcible feeding, which we request to be stopped without any further delay

In addition, we may be permitted to refer to the recommendations made in the U.P. Jail Committee by Pt. Jagat Narain and K.B. Hafiz Hidayat Hussain. They have recommended the political prisoners to be treated as "Better Class Prisoners". We request you to kindly consider our demands at your earliest convenience.

By "Political Prisoners", we mean all those people who are convicted for offences against the State, for instance the people who were convicted in the Lahore Conspiracy Cases, 1915-17, the Kakori Conspiracy Cases and Sedition Cases in general.

Yours,

Bhagat Singh
B. K. Dutt

7

Reiterating Hunger-Strikers' Demands

28 January 1930

After suspending hunger strike on assurance of consideration, the government retorted to some kind of delay or the other There was also some disciplinary action taken against participants in the strike, which led Bhagat Singh to write this letter

"*If you oppose a prevailing belief, if you criticize a great person who is considered to be an incarnation, you will find that your criticism will be answered by calling you vain and egoist.*"

– Bhagat Singh

The Home Member,
The Govt, of India
Delhi.

Through
The Special Magistrate,
Lahore Conspiracy Case,
Lahore.

Sir,

With reference to our telegram dated 20th Jan, 1930, reading as follows, we have not been given any reply.

Home Member Government. Delhi Under trials, Lahore Conspiracy Case and other Political Prisoners suspended hunger strike on the assurance that the India Govt, was considering Provincial Jail Committee's reports. All Government Conference over. No action yet taken. As vindictive treatment to political prisoners still continues, we request we be informed within a week final Govt, decision. Lahore Conspiracy Case under trials.

As briefly stated in the above telegram, we beg to bring to your kind notice that the Lahore Conspiracy Case under trials and several other political prisoners confined in Punjab jails suspended hunger strike on the assurance given by the members of the Punjab Jail Enquiry Committee that the question of the treatment of political prisoners was going to be finally settled to our satisfaction within a very short period. Further, after the death of our great martyr Jatindra Nath Das, the matter was taken up in the Legislative Assembly and the same assurance was given publicly by Sir James Crerap. It was then pronounced that there has been a change of heart and the question of the treatment of political prisoners was receiving the utmost sympathy of the government. Such political prisoners who were still on hunger strike in jails of the different parts of the country then suspended their hunger strike on the request being made to this effect in an AICC resolution passed in view of the said assurance and the critical condition of some of the prisoners.

Since then, all the local governments have submitted their reports. A meeting of Inspectors-General of Prisons of different provinces has been held at Lucknow and the deliberations of the All-India Government Conference have been concluded at Delhi. The All-India Conference was held in the month of December last, but not carried into effect any final recommendations. By such dilatory attitude of the government, we no less than the general public have begun to fear that perhaps the question has been shelved. Our apprehensions have been strengthened by the vindictive treatment meted out to hunger strikers and other political prisoners during the last four months. It is very difficult for us to know the details of the hardships to which the political prisoners are being subjected. Still the little information that has trickled out of the four walls of the jails in sufficient to furnish us with glaring instances. We give below a few such instances which we cannot but feel, are not in conformity with the government's assurance.

(1) Sh. B.K. Banerji, undergoing five years imprisonment in connection with Dakshineshwar Bomb Case in Lahore Central Jail, joined the hunger strike last year. Now as a punishment for the same, for each day of his period of hunger strike, two days of the remission so far earned by him have been forfeited. Under usual circumstances his release was due in December last, but it will be delayed by full four months. In the same Jail, similar punishment has been awarded to Baba Sohan Singh, an old man of about seventy, now undergoing his sentence of life transportation in connection with the (first) Lahore Conspiracy Case. Besides, among others, Sardar Gopal Singh confined in Mianwali Jail, Master Mota Singh confined in Rawalpindi Jail have also been awarded vindictive punishments for joining the general hunger strike. In most of these cases, the periods of imprisonment have been enhanced while some of them have been removed from the Special class.

(2) For the same offence, i.e. joining the general hunger strike, Messrs. Sachindra Nath Sanyal, Ram Kishan Khattri and Suresh Chandra Bhattacharya, confined in Agra Central Jail, Raj Kumar Sinha, Sachindra Nath Bukshi, Manmath Nath Gupta and several other Kakori case prisoners have been severely punished. It is reliably learnt that Mr. Sanyal was given bar-fetters and solitary cell-confinement and as a consequence, there has been a break-down in his health. His weight has gone down

by eighteen pounds. Mr. Bhattacharya is reported to be suffering from tuberculosis. The three Bareilly Jail prisoners also have been punished. It is learnt that all their privileges have been withdrawn. Even their usual rights of interviewing with relations and communication with them were forfeited. They have all been considerably reduced in their weights. Two press statements have been issued in this connection in September 1929 and January 1930 by Pandit Jawaharlal Nehru.

(3) After the passing of the AICC resolution regarding hunger strike, the copies of the same, which were sent to different political prisoners, were withheld by the jail authorities. Further, the government refused a Congress deputation to meet the prisoners in this respect.

(4) The Lahore Conspiracy Case under trials were assaulted brutally on 23rd and 24th October, 1929, by orders of high police officials. Full details have appeared in the press. The copy of the statement of one of us recorded by the Special Magistrate, Pt. Shri Krishan, has been duly forwarded to you in a communication dated 16th December, 1929. Neither the Punjab Government, nor the Government of India felt it necessary to reply or even acknowledge receipt of our communication, praying for an enquiry. While, on the other hand, local government has felt the imperative necessity of prosecuting us in connection with the very same incident for offering Violent' resistance,

(5) In the last week of December, 1929, Sj. Kiran Chandra Das and eight others confined in the Lahore Borstal Jail,

when being taken to and produced in the Magistrates Court, were found handcuffed and chained together in flagrant breach of the unanimous recommendations of the Punjab Jail Enquiry Committee and also of Inspector-General of Prisons, Punjab. It is further noteworthy that these prisoners were under trials, changed for a bailable offence. A long statement issued by Dr. Mohd. Aslam, Lala Duni Chand of Lahore and Lala Duni Chand of Ambala in this connection was published in *Tribune*.

When we learnt these and other sufferings of the political prisoners, we refrained from resuming our hunger strike, though we were much grieved as we thought that the matter was going to be finally settled at an early date, but in the light of the above instances, are we now to believe that the untold sufferings of the hunger strikers and the supreme sacrifice made by Jatin Das have all been in vain? Are we to understand that the government gave its assurance only to check the growing tide of public agitation and to avert a crisis? You will agree with us if we say that we have waited patiently for a sufficiently reasonable period of time. But we cannot wait indefinitely. The government, by its dilatory attitude and the continuation of vindictive treatment to political prisoners, has left us no other option but to resume the struggle. We realize that to go on hunger strike and to carry it on is no easy task. But let us at the same time point out that India can produce many more Jatins and Wagias, Ran Rakshas and Bhan Singhs. (The last two named laid down their lives in the Andamans in 1917 - the first breathed his last after 63 days of hunger strike while the other died the death of a great hero after silently undergoing in human tortures for full six months.)

Enough has been said by us and the members of the
public (inquiry committee) in justification of the better
treatment of political prisoners and it is unnecessary here
to repeat the same. We would however like to say a few
words as regards the inclusion of motive as the basis and
the most important factor in the matter of classification.
Great fuss has been created on the question of criteria of
classification. We find that motive has altogether been
excluded so far from the criteria suggested by different
provincial governments This is really strange attitude.
It is through motive alone that the real value of any
action can be decided. Are we to understand that the
government is unable to distinguish between a robber
who robs and kills his victim and a Kharag Bahadur
who kills a villain and saves the honour of a young lady
and redeems society of a most licentious parasite? Are
both to be treated as two men belonging to the same
category? Is there no difference between two men who
commit the same offence, one guided by selfish motive
and the other by a selfless one? Similarly, is there no
difference between a common murderer and a political
worker, even if the latter resorts to violence? Does not
his selflessness elevate his place from amongst those of
ordinary criminals? In these circumstances we think that
motive should be held as the most important factor in
the criteria for classification.

Last year, in the beginning of our hunger strike,
when public leaders including Dr. Gopi Chand and Lala
Duni Chand of Ambala - the last named being one of
the signatories to the Punjab Jail Enquiry Committee
Report - approached us to discuss the same thing and
when they told us that the government considered to

treat the political prisoners convicted of offences of violent nature as Special Class prisoners, then by way of compromise we agreed to the proposal to the extent of excluding those actually charged with murder. But, later on, the discussion took a different turn and the communique containing the terms of reference for the Punjab Jail Enquiry Committee was so worded that the question of motive seemed to be altogether excluded, and the classification was based on two thing:

(1) Nature of Offence; and
(2) Social Status of "Offender".

These criteria, instead of solving the problem, made it all the more complicated.

We could understand two classes amongst the political prisoners, those charged for non-violent offences and those charged for violent offences. But then creeps in the question of social status in the report of the Punjab Jail Enquiry Committee. As Chaudhary Afzal Haque has pointed out, and rightly too, in his note of dissent to this report, what will be the fate of those political workers who have been reduced to pauper's conditions due to their honorary services in the cause of freedom? Are they to be left at the mercy of a magistrate who will try to prove the bonafide of his loyalty by classifying everyone as an ordinary convict? Or, is it expected that a non-cooperator will stretch his hand before the people against whom he is fighting as an opponent, begging for better treatment in jail? Is this the way of removing the causes of dissatisfaction, or rather intensifying them? It might be argued that people living in property outside the jails, should not expect luxuries inside the prison when they are detained for the purpose of punishment. But, are the reforms that are demanded, of a nature of luxury? Are they not the bare necessities of life, according to the most moderate standard of living? In spite of all the facilities that can possibly be demanded, jail will ever remain a jail. The prison in itself does not contain and can never contain any magnetic power to attract the people from outside. Nobody will commit offences simply to come to jail. Moreover, may we venture to say that it is a very poor argument on the part of any government to say that its citizens have been driven to such extreme destitution that their standard of living has fallen even lower than that of jails? Does not such an argument cut at the very root of that government's right of existence? Anyhow, we are not concerned with that at present. What we want to say is that the best way to remove the prevailing dissatisfaction would be to classify the political prisoners as such into a separate class which may further be subdivided, if need be, into two classes – one for those convicted of non-violent offences and the other for persons whose offences include violence. In that case, motive will become one of the deciding factors. To say that motive cannot be ascertained in political cases is hypocritical assertion. What is it that today informs the jail authorities to deprive the 'political' even of the ordinary privileges? What it is that deprives them of the special grades or 'nambardaries', etc.? What makes the authorities to keep them aloof and separated from all other convicts? The same thing can help in the classification also.

As for the special demands, we have already stated them in full in our memorandum to the Punjab Jail

Enquiry Committee. We would however particularly emphasize that no political

prisoner, whatever his offence may be, should be given any hard and undignified labour for which he may not feel aptitude. All of them, confined in one jail, should be kept together in the same ward. At least one standard daily newspaper in vernacular or English should be given to them. Full and proper facilities for study should be granted. Lastly, they should be allowed to supplement their expenses for diet and clothing from their private sources.

We still hope that the government will carry into effect without further delay its promise made to us and to the public, so that there may not be another occasion for resuming the hunger strike. Unless and until we find a definite move on the part of the government to redeem its promise in the course of the next seven days, we shall be forced to resume the hunger strike.

Yours,
Bhagat Singh, Dutt, others
Dated :28th Jan., 1930
Under trials, Lahore Conspiracy Case

8

Message to Punjab Students' Conference

19 October 1929

Bhagat Singh wrote this message jointly with B.K. Dutt for the students attending the second Punjab Students' Conference, under the presidentship of Subhas Chandra Bose, to inspire them to fight for the nation wholeheartedly.

"Revolution was the vital living force indicative of eternal conflict between life and death, the old and the new, light and the darkness"

– Bhagat Singh

Comrades

Today, we cannot ask the youth to take to pistols and bombs. Today, students are confronted with a far more important assignment. In the coming Lahore Session, the Congress is to give call for a fierce fight for the independence of the country. The youth will have to bear a great burden in these difficult times in the history of the nation. It is true that students have faced death at the forward positions of the struggle for independence. Will they hesitate this time in proving their same staunchness and self-confidence? The youth will have to spread this revolutionary message to the far corner of the country. They have to awaken crores of slum-dwellers of the industrial areas and villagers living in worn-out cottages, so that we will be independent and the exploitation of man by man will become an impossibility. Punjab is considered politically backward even otherwise. This is also the responsibility of the youth. Taking inspiration from the martyr Yatindra Nath Das and with boundless reverence for the country, they must prove that they can fight with steadfast resolve in this struggle for independence.

9

When Sukhdev Thought of Suicide

1930

Sukhdev wrote a letter to Bhagat Singh, mentioning that he would be willing to kill himself if he was sentenced to life imprisonment instead of execution. This was Bhagat Singh's response to it.

"Any man who stands for progress has to criticize, disbelieve and challenge every item of the old faith."

– Bhagat Singh

Dear Brother,

I have gone through your letter attentively and many times. I realize that the changed situation has affected us differently. The things you hated outside have now become essential to you. In the same way, the things I used to support strongly are of no significance to me anymore. For example, I believed in personal love, but now this feeling has ceased to occupy any particular position in my heart and mind. While outside, you were strongly opposed to it, but now a drastic change and radicalization is apparent in your ideas about it. You experience it as an extremely essential part of human existence and you have found a particular kind of happiness in the experience.

You may still recollect that one day I had discussed suicide with you. That time I told you that in some situations, suicide may be justifiable, but you contested my point. I vividly remember the time and place of our conversation. We talked about this in the Shahanshahi Kutia one evening. You said in jest that such a cowardly act can never be justified. You said that acts of this kind were horrible and heinous, but I see that you have now made an about-turn on this subject. Now you find it not only proper in certain situations, but also necessary, even essential. My opinion is what you had held earlier, that suicide is a heinous crime. It is an act of complete cowardice. Leave alone revolutionaries, no individual can ever justify such an act.

You say you fail to understand how suffering alone can serve the country. Such a question from a person like you is really perplexing, because how thoughtfully we loved the motto of the Naujawan Bharat Sabha - "to suffer and sacrifice through service". I believe that you served as much as was possible. Now is the time when you should suffer for what you did. Another point is that this is exactly the moment when you have to lead the entire people.

Man acts only when he is sure of the justness of his action, as we threw the bomb in the Legislative Assembly. After the action, it is the time for bearing the consequences of that act. Do you think that had we tried to avoid the punishment by pleading for mercy, we would have been more justified? No, this would have had an adverse effect on the masses. We are now quite successful in our endeavour.

At the time of our imprisonment, the conditions for the political prisoners of our party were very miserable. We tried to improve that. I told you quite seriously that we believed we would die very shortly. Neither we were aware of the technique of forced feeding, nor did we ever think of it. We were ready to die. Do you mean to say that we were intending to commit suicide? No. Striving and sacrificing one's life for a superior ideal can never be called suicide. We are envious of the death of our comrade Yatindra Nath Das. Will you call it suicide? Ultimately, our sufferings bore fruit. A big movement started in the whole of the country. We were successful in our aim. Death in the struggles of this kind is an ideal death.

Apart from this, the comrades among us, who believe that they will be awarded death, should await that day patiently when the sentence will be announced and they will be hanged. This death will also be beautiful, but committing suicide - to cut short the life just to avoid some pain - is cowardice. I want to tell you that obstacles make a man perfect. Neither you nor I, rather none of us, have suffered any pain so far. That part of our life has started only now. You will recollect that we have talked several times about realism in the Rusian literature, which is nowhere visible in our own. We highly appreciate the situations of pain in their stories, but we do not feel that spirit of suffering within ourselves. We also admire their passion and the extraordinary height of their characters, but we never bother to find out the reason. I will say that only the reference to their resolve to bear pain has produced the intensity, the suffering of pain, and this has given great depth and height to their characters and literature. We become pitiable and ridiculous when we imbibe an unreasoned mysticism in our life without any natural or substantial basis. People like us, who are proud to be revolutionary in every sense, should always be prepared to bear all the difficulties, anxieties, pain and suffering which we invite upon ourselves by the struggles initiated by us and for which we call ourselves revolutionary.

I want to tell you, that in jail, and in jail alone, can a person get an occasion to study empirically the great social subjects of crime and sin. I have read some literature on this and only the jail is the proper place for self-study on all these topics. The best parts of the self-study for one is to suffer oneself.

You know it that the suffering of political prisoners in the jails of Russia caused, in the main, the revolution in the prison-administration after the overthrow of Czardom. Is India not in need of such persons who are fully aware of this problem and have personal experience of these things? It will not suffice to say that someone else would do it, or that many other people are there to do it. Thus, men who find it quite dishonourable and hateful to leave the revolutionary responsibilities to others should start their struggle against the existing system with total devotion. They should violate these rules, but they should also keep in mind the propriety, because unnecessary and improper attempts can never be considered just. Such agitations will shorten the process of revolution. All the arguments which you gave to keep yourself aloof from all such movement, are incomprehensible to me. Some of our friends are either fools or ignorant. They find your behaviour quite strange and incomprehensible. (They themselves say they cannot comprehend it because you are above and very far from their understanding.)

In fact, if you feel that jail life is really humiliating, why don't you try to improve it by agitating? Perhaps, you will say that this struggle would be futile, but this is precisely the argument which is usually used as a cover by weak people to avoid participation in every movement. This is the reply which we kept on hearing outside the jail from the people who were anxious to escape from getting entangled in revolutionary movements. Shall I now hear the same argument from you? What could our party of a handful of people do in comparison to the vastness of its aims and ideals? Shall we infer from this that we erred gravely in starting our work altogether? No, inferences of this kind will be improper. This only shows the inner weakness of the man who thinks like this. You write further that it cannot be expected of a man that he will have the same thinking after going through 14 long years of suffering in the prison, which he had before, because the jail life will crush all his ideas. May I ask you whether the situation outside the jail was any bit more favourable to our ideas? Even then, could we have left it because of our failures? Do you mean to imply that had we not entered the field, no revolutionary work would have taken place at all? If this be your contention, then you are mistaken, though it is right that we also proved helpful to an extent in changing the environment. But, we are only a product of the need of our times.

I shall even say that Marx – the father of communism – did not actually originate this idea. The Industrial Revolution of Europe itself produced men of this kind. Marx was one among them. Of course, Marx was also instrumental to an extent in gearing up the wheels of his time in a particular way.

I (and you too) did not give birth to the ideas of socialism and communism in this country; this is the consequence of the effects of our time and situations upon ourselves. Of course, we did a bit to propagate these ideas, and therefore I say that since we have already taken a tough task upon ourselves, we should continue to advance it. The people will not be guided by our committing suicides to escape the difficulties; on the contrary, this will be quite a reactionary step.

We continued our work despite the testing environment of disappointments, pressures and violence ordained by the jail rules. While we worked, we were made target of many kinds of difficulties. Even men who were proud to proclaim themselves to be great revolutionaries, deserted us. Were these conditions not testing in the extreme? Then, what was the reason and the logic of continuing our agitation and efforts?

Does this simple argument not by itself give added strength to our ideas? And, don't we have instances of our revolutionary comrades who suffered for their convictions in jails and are still working on return from jails? Had Bakunin argued like you, he would have committed suicide right in the beginning. Today, you find many revolutionaries occupying responsible posts in the Russian state who had passed the greater part of their lives in prison, completing their sentences. Man must try hard to stick to his beliefs. No one can say what future has in store.

Do you remember when we were discussing that some concentrated and effective poison should also be kept in our bomb factories, you opposed it very vehemently. The very idea was repugnant to you. You had no faith in it. So, what has happened now? Here, even the difficult and complex conditions do not obtain. I feel revulsion even in discussing this question. You hated even that attitude of mind which permits suicide. You will kindly excuse me for saying that had you acted according to this belie right at the time of your imprisonment (that is, you had committed suicide by taking poison), you would have served the revolutionary cause, but at this moment, even the thought of such an act is harmful to our cause.

There is just one more point which I would like to draw your attention to. We do not believe in god, hell and heaven, punishment and rewards, that is in any godly accounting of human life. Therefore, we must think of life and death on materialist lines. When I was brought here from Delhi for the purpose of identification, some intelligence officers talked to me on this topic, in the presence of my father. They said that since I did not try to save my life by divulging secrets, it proved the presence of an acute agony in my life. They argued that a death of this kind will be something like suicide. But I had replied that a man with beliefs and ideal like mine, could never think of dying uselessly. We want to get the maximum value for our lives. We want to serve humanity as much as possible. Particularly a man like me, whose life is nowhere sad or worried, can never even think of suicide, leave alone attempting it. The same thing I want to tell you now.

I hope you will permit me to tell you what I think about myself. I am certain of capital punishment for me. I do not expect even a bit of moderation or amnesty. Even if there is amnesty, it will not be for all, and even that amnesty will be for others only, not for us; it will be extremely restricted and burdened with various conditions. For us, neither can there be any amnesty, nor will it ever happen. Even then, I wish that release calls for us should be made collection and globally. Along with that, I also wish that when the movement reaches its climax, we should be hanged. It is my wish that if at any time any honourable and fair compromise is possible, issue like our case may never obstruct it. When the fate of the country is being decided, the fate of individuals should be forgotten. As revolutionaries, we do not believe that there can be any sudden change in the attitude of our rulers, particularly in the British race. Such a surprising change is impossible without thorough sustained striving, sufferings and sacrifices. And it shall be achieved. As far as my attitude is concerned, I can welcome facilities and amnesty for all only when its effect is permanent and some indelible impressions are made on the hearts of the people of the country through our hanging. Only this much and nothing more.

10

On Why He Refused to Attend Court

1930

After their second hunger strike, the prisoners were assured of fulfillment of their demands, but several other minor ones were sidelined. Following that, Bhagat Singh refused to attend court. When a local daily explained this as their boycott of the British courts, Bhagat Singh wrote the following.

"*The aim of life is no more to control the mind, but to develop it harmoniously; not to achieve salvation here after, but to make the best use of it here below...*"

- Bhagat Singh

Mister Magistrate,

After going through your order dated 4 February, 1930, which was published in *The Civil* and *Military Gazette*, it appears necessary that we explain to you the reason of our boycott of the court.

It is wrong to say that we have boycotted the courts of the British government. Today, we are going to the court of Mr. Louis who is hearing the case initiated against us under Section 22 of the Jail Act. We had presented our problems and difficulties in our bail application before you, but it still remains unconsidered.

Our comrades under trial belong to different and distant corners of the country. Therefore, they should be given the facility of meeting their well wishers and sympathizers. Shri B.K. Dutt gave an application to meet Miss Lajjawati, and Shri Kamal Nath Tewari also wanted to meet someone, but were neither their relatives nor their lawyers. Even after securing their authorization, they were not allowed to meet. It is quite clear from this that the under trials are not given the facilities for their defense. Not merely this, Comrade Kranti Kumar, who was doing very useful work for our defense committee and was also providing us with things of daily use, has been imprisoned on a fabricated charge. It has come to our knowledge that the fabricated charge of bringing bullets in the sauce could not be proved against him, under Section 124 A in Gurudaspur, which is distant from Lahore.

I myself cannot keep a whole time lawyer, therefore I wanted that my trusted friends should observe the court proceedings by being present there. But they were denied permission without any explicit reason, and only Lala Amardas, Advocate, has been given a seat.

We can never like this drama acted in the name of justice, because we do not get any facility or benefit for defending ourselves. One more serious complaint is against non-available newspapers. Under trial prisoners cannot be treated like convicted prisoners. We should be given at least one newspaper regularly We want one newspaper also for those who do not know English. Therefore, as a protest, we are returning even the English daily *Tribune*. We decided to boycott the court on 29 January, 1930, because of these complaints. We will rejoin the proceedings when these inconveniences are removed.

11

Regarding the LCC Ordinance

2 May 1930

In the face of recurrent and active hunger strikes by the accused in Lahore Conspiracy Case, the Government of India passed an ordinance called LCC Ordinance No. 3 of 1930, which allowed for the establishment of a Special Tribunal comprising three high court judges, who could carry on the court proceedings even in the absence of the accused. This letter was written by Bhagat Singh as a response to the Governor-General of India's support to the ordinance.

"If the deaf are to hear, then sound has to be very loud."

\- Bhagat Singh

To

His Excellency
The Governor-General of India
Simla.
2nd May, 1930

Sir,

The full text of the special ordinance to expedite our trial has been read over to us. To Tribunal has also been appointed by the Chief Justice of the Punjab High Court of Juridicature. We welcome the news. We could have kept silent, had you not referred to our attitude adopted so far in this case, and thus tried to throw the sole responsibility on our shoulders. In the present situation, we feel it necessary to make a statement to clear our position.

We have been marking from the very beginning that the government authorities have always been trying to deliberately misrepresent us. After all, this is a fight, and the misrepresentation is and has always been the best instrument in the hands of the government to meet their enemies. We have absolutely no grudge against this mean tactic. However, there are certain things the consideration of which is forcing us to make the following counter.

You have mentioned in your statement issued alongwith the Lahore Conspiracy Ordinance, our hunger strike. As you have yourself admitted, two of us had begun the hunger strike weeks before the commencement of the inquiry into this case in the court of R.S Pt. Sri Krishan, Special Magistrate. Hence any man with the least common sense can understand that the hunger strike had nothing to do with the trial. The government had to admit the existence of these grievances. When the government made some gesture as to making certain arrangement for the settlement of this question, and Provincial Jail Enquiry Committees were appointed for the same purpose, we gave up the hunger strike. But at first we were informed that the question would be finally settled in November. Then it was postponed till December. But January also passed and there was not the least to indicate as to whether the government was going to the do anything in this connection at all, or not. We feared that the matter was shelved. Hence the second hunger; strike on 4th Feb., 1930, after full one weeks notice. It was only then that the government tried to settle this question finally. A Communique was published and we again gave up the hunger strike and did not even wait to see the final decision, in this connection, carried into effect. It is only today that we are realizing that the British government has not yet given up the policy of telling lies even in such ordinary matters as this. This Communique is in specific terms, but we find something quite contrary in practice. Anyhow, this is not the proper place to discuss that question; we might have to deal with it later on, if the occasion arises. But what we want to emphasize here is that the hunger strike was never directed against the proceedings of the court. Such great sufferings cannot be invited and such great sacrifice cannot be made with that ordinary motive. Das did not lay down his life for such a trivial cause. Rajguru and others did not risk their lives simply to protract the trial.

You know thoroughly well, and everybody concerned knows it, that it is not the hunger strike that has forced you to promulgate this Ordinance. There is something else, the consideration of which confused the heads of your government; it is neither the protraction of the case nor any other emergency which forces you to sign this lawless law. It is certainly something different.

But let us declare once and for all that our spirits cannot be cowed down by ordinances. You may crush certain individuals, but you cannot crush this nation. As far as this Ordinance is concerned, we consider it to be our victory. We had been from the very beginning pointing out that this existing law was a mere make-believe. It could not administer justice. But even those privileges to which the accused were legitimately and legally entitled and which are given to ordinary accused were legitimately and legally entitled and which are given to ordinary accused, could not be given to the accused in political cases. We wanted to make the government throw off its veil and to be candid enough to admit that fair chances for defense could not be given to the political accused. Here we have the frank admission of the government. We congratulate you as well as your government for this candour and welcome the Ordinance.

In spite of the frank admission of your agents, the Special Magistrate and the Prosecution Counsels, as to the reasonableness of our attitude throughout, you had been confused at the very thought of the existence of our case. What else is needed to assure us of our success in this fight.

12

Letter to Jaidev Gupta

24 July 1930

Bhagat Singh requested his close friend from school to send over some books for him.

"*Let me announce, with all the strength at my command, that I am not a terrorist and I never was, expect perhaps in the beginning of my revolutionary career And I am convinced that we cannot gain anything through those methods.*"

– Bhagat Singh

Lahore Central Jail
24th July, 1930

My dear Jaidev,

P lease take following books in my name from
Dwarkadas Library and send them through
Kulvir on Sunday:

Militarism (Karl Liebknecht)
Why Men Fight (B. Russel)
Soviets at Work.
Collapse of the Second International
Left-Wing Communism
Mutual Aid (Prince Kropotkin)
Fields, Factories and Workshops
Civil War in France (Marx)
Land Revolution in Russia
Spy (Upton Sinclair)

Please send one more book from Punjab Public
Library: *Historical Materialism (Bukharin)*. Also, please
find out from the librarian if some books have been sent
to Borstal Jail. They are facing a terrible famine of books.
They had sent a list of books through Sukhdev's brother
Jaidev. They have not received any book till now. In case
they have no list, then please ask Lala Firoz Chand to
send some interesting books of his choice. The books

must reach them before I go there on this Sunday. This work is a must. Please keep this in mind.

Also send *Punjab Peasants in Prosperity and Debt* by Darling and 2 or 3 books of this type for Dr. Alam. Hope you will excuse me for this trouble. I promise I will not trouble you in future. Please remember me to all my friends and convey my respect to Lajjawati. I am sure if Dutt's sister came, she will not forget to see me.

With regards,

Bhagat Singh

13

For the Removal of Justice Hilton

25 June 1930

The presiding judge on the Lahore Conspiracy Case lost his temper during the proceedings, and got the accused handcuffed, and sent back to jail. As retaliation, Bhagat Singh asked for the judge to be removed. On 21 June, the presiding judge was removed, but instead of the next senior judge – who was sympathetic towards the accused –Justice Hilton, was appointed in his place – who was a party to the order. The accused objected to it and Bhagat Singh wrote this letter.

"I never had any desire to defend myself, and never did I seriously think about it."

- Bhagat Singh

To

The Commissioner,
The Special Tribunal, Lahore Conspiracy Case,
Lahore

Sir,

Whereas two judges of the Tribunal have withdrawn or have been made to withdraw themselves from the Tribunal and two new judges have been appointed in their place, we feel that a statement is very necessary on our part to explain our position clearly so that no misunderstanding may be possible.

It was on 12th May, 1930, that an order was passed by Mr. Justice Coldstream, the then President, to handcuff us. In asking the court to inform us as to the cause of this sudden and extraordinary order was not thought worth consideration. The police handcuffed us forcibly and removed us back to jail. One of the three judges, Mr. Agha Harider, on the following day, dissociated himself with that order of the President. Since that day, we have not been attending court.

Our condition on which we were prepared to attend court was laid before the Tribunal on the next day, namely that either the President should apologize or he should be replaced; by this we never meant that a judge who was a party to that order should take the place of the President.

For more than five weeks, no heed was paid to the grievances of the accused.

According to the present formation of the Tribunal, both the President and the other judge who had dissociated himself from the order of the President, have been replaced by two new judges. Thus the judge who was a party to that order - as the President gave the order on behalf of the majority - has now been appointed the President of the Tribunal. In these circumstances, we want to emphasize one thing that we had absolutely no grudge against the person of Mr. Justice Coldstream. We had protested against the order passed by the President on behalf of the majority and the subsequent maltreatment meted out to us. We have every respect for Mr. Justice Coldstream and Mr. Justice Hilton that should be expected from man to man. And as our protest was against a certain order, we wanted the President to apologize, which meant apology by the President on behalf of the Tribunal who was responsible for that order. By the removal of the President, the Position is not changed because Mr. Justice Hilton, who was a party to the order, is presiding in place, position has added an insult to injury.

Yours, etc.
Bhagat Singh, B.K. Dutt

14

Letter to B.K. Dutt

November, 1930

After the death sentence was pronounced for him, he wrote down his feelings to his comrade.

'I will climb the gallows gladly and show to the world as to how bravely the revolutionaries can sacrifice themselves for the cause."

- Bhagat Singh

Central Jail,
November, 1930

Dear Brother,

The judgment has been delivered. I am condemned to death. In these cells, besides myself, there are many others prisoners who are waiting to be hanged. The only prayer of these people is that somehow or other they may escape the noose. Perhaps I am the only man amongst them who is anxiously waiting for the day when I will be fortunate enough to embrace the gallows for my idcal.

I will climb the gallows gladly and show to the world as to how bravely the revolutionaries can sacrifice themselves for the cause.

I will be condemned to death, but you are sentenced to transportation for life. You will live and, while living, you will have to show to the world that the revolutionaries not only die for their ideals, but can face every calamity. Death should not be a means to escape the worldly difficulties. Those revolutionaries who have by chance escaped the gallows for the ideal but also bear the worst type of tortures in the dark dingy prison cells.

Yours,
Bhagat Singh

15

To Young Political Workers

2 February 1931

After Bhagat Singh's execution, this document was published in a mutilated form. All references to Soviet Union, Marx, Lenin and the Communist Party were carefully deleted. Subsequently, the Government of India published it in one of its secret reports in 1936.

"Study was the cry that reverberated in the corridors of my mind. Study to enable yourself to face the arguments advanced by opposition. Study to arm yourself with arguments in favor of your cult. I began to study."

– Bhagat Singh

To

The Young Political Workers.

Dear Comrades

Our movement is passing through a very important phase at present. After a year's fierce struggle, some definite proposals regarding the constitutional reforms have been formulated by the Round Table Conference and the Congress leaders have been invited to give this... think it desirable in the present circumstances to call off their movement. Whether they decide in favour or against is a matter of little importance to us. The present movement is bound to end in some sort of compromise. The compromise may be effected sooner or later. And compromise is not such ignoble and deplorable a thing as we generally think. It is rather an indispensable factor in the political strategy. Any nation that rises against the oppressors is bound to fail in the beginning, and to gain partial reforms during the medieval period of its struggle through compromises. And it is only at the last stage - having fully organized all the forces and resources of the nation - that it can possibly strike the final blow in which it might succeed to shatter the ruler's government. But even then it might fail, which makes some sort of compromise inevitable. This can be best illustrated by the Russian example.

In 1905 a revolutionary movement broke out in Russia. All the leaders were very hopeful. Lenin had returned from the foreign countries where he had taken refuge. He was conducting the struggle. People came to tell him that a dozen landlords were killed and a score of their mansions were burnt. Lenin responded by telling them to return and to kill twelve hundred landlords and burn as many of their palaces. In his opinion, that would have meant something if revolution failed. Duma was introduced. The same Lenin advocated the view of participating in the Duma. This is what happened in 1907. In 1906 he was opposed to the participation in this first Duma which had granted more scope of work than this second one, whose rights had been curtailed. This was due to the changed circumstances. Reaction was gaining the upper hand and Lenin wanted to use the floor of the Duma as a platform to discuss socialist ideas.

Again after the 1917 revolution, when the Bolsheviks were forced to sign the Brest Litovsk Treaty, everyone except Lenin was opposed to it. But Lenin said: "Peace". "Peace and again peace: peace at any cost - even at the cost of many of the Russian provinces to be yielded to German War Lord". When some anti-Bolshevik people condemned Lenin for this treaty, he declared frankly that the Bolsheviks were not in a position to face German onslaught and they preferred the treaty to the complete annihilation of the Bolshevik Government.

The thing that I wanted to point out was that compromise is an essential weapon which has to be wielded every now and then as the struggle develops. But the thing that we must keep always before us is the idea of the movement. We must always maintain a clear

notion as to the aim for the achievement of which we are
fighting. That helps us to verify the success and failures
of our movements and we can easily formulate the future
programme. Tilak's policy, quite apart from the ideal, i.e.
his strategy, was the best. You are fighting to get sixteen
annas from your enemy, you get only one anna. Pocket it
and fight for the rest. What we note in the moderates is
of their ideal. They start to achieve on anna and they can't
get it. The revolutionaries must always keep in mind that
they are striving for a complete revolution. Complete
mastery of power in their hands. Compromises are
dreaded because the conservatives try to disband the
revolutionary forces after the compromise from such
pitfalls. We must be very careful at such junctures to
avoid any sort of confusion of the real issues, especially
the goal. The British Labour leaders betrayed their
real struggle and have been reduced to mere hypocrite
imperialists. In my opinion, the diehard conservatives
are better to us than these polished imperialist Labour
leaders. About the tactics and strategy, one should study
life-work of Lenin. His definite views on the subject of
compromise will be found in "Left Wing" Communism.

I have said that the present movement, i.e. the present
struggle, is bound to end in some sort of compromise or
complete failure.

I said that, because in my opinion, this time the
real revolutionary forces have not been invited into the
arena. This is a struggle dependent upon the middle
class shopkeepers and a few capitalists. Both these, and
particularly the latter, can never dare to risk its property or
possessions in any struggle. The real revolutionary armies
are in the villages and in factories, the peasantry and the

labourers. But our bourgeois leaders do not and cannot dare to tackle them. The sleeping lion once awakened from its slumber shall become irresistible even after the achievement of what our leaders aim at. After his first experience with the Ahmedabad labourers in 1920, Mahatma Gandhi declared, "We must not tamper with the labourers. It is dangerous to make political use of the factory proletariat" *(The Times,* May 1921). Since then, they never dared to approach them. There remains the peasantry. The Bardoli resolution of 1922 clearly denies the horror the leaders felt when they saw the gigantic peasant class rising to shake off not only the domination of an alien nation, but also the yoke of the landlords.

It is there that our leaders prefer a surrender to the British than to the peasantry. Leave alone Pt. Jawaharlal. Can you point out any effort to organize the peasants or the labourers? No, they will not run the risk. There they lack. That is why I say they never meant a complete revolution. Through economic and administrative pressure, they hoped to get a few more reforms, a few more concessions for the Indian capitalists. That is why I say that this movement is doomed to die, may be after some sort of compromise or even without. They young workers who in all sincerity raise the cry "Inquilab Zindabad", are not well organized and strong enough to carry the movement themselves. As a matter of fact, even our great leaders, with the exception of perhaps Pt. Motilal Nehru, do not dare to take any responsibility on their shoulders, that is why every now and then they surrender unconditionally before Gandhi. In spite of their differences, they never oppose him seriously and the resolutions have to be carried for the Mahatma.

In these circumstances, let me warn the sincere young workers who seriously mean a revolution, that harder times are coming. Let them beware, lest they should get confused or disheartened. After the experience made through two struggles of the Great Gandhi, we are in a better position to form a clear idea of our present position and the future programme.

Now allow me to state the case in the simplest manner. You cry "Long Live the Revolution". Let me assume that you really mean it. According to our definition of the term, as stated in our statement in the Assembly Bomb Case, revolution means the complete overthrow of the existing social order and its replacement with the socialist order. For that purpose, our immediate aim is the achievement of power. As a matter of fact, the state, the government machinery is just a weapon in the hands of the ruling class to further and safeguard its interest. We want to snatch and handle it to utilise it for the consummation of our ideal basis, i.e. social reconstruction on new, i.e. Marxist. For this purpose we are fighting to handle the government machinery. All along we have to educate the masses and to create a favourable atmosphere for our social programme. In the struggles, we can best train and educate them.

With these things clear before us, i.e. our immediate and ultimate object having been clearly put, we can now proceed with the examination of the present situation. We must always be very candid and quite business-like while analysing any situation. We know that since a hue and cry was raised about the Indians' participation in and share in the responsibility of the Indian government, the Minto-Morley Reforms were introduced, which formed the Viceroys council with consultation rights only. During the Great War, when the Indian help was needed the most, promises about self-government were made and the existing reforms were introduced. Limited legislative powers have been entrusted to the Assembly, but subject to the goodwill of the Viceroy. Now is the third stage.

Now reforms are being discussed and are to be introduced in the near future. How can our young men judge them? This is a question. I do not know by what standard are the Congress leaders going to judge them. But for us, the revolutionaries, we can have the following criteria:

1. Extent of responsibility transferred to the shoulders of the Indians.
2. From of the government institutions that are going to be introduced and the extent of the right of participation given to the masses.
3. Future prospects and the safeguards.

These might require a little further elucidation. In the first place, we can easily judge the extent of responsibility given to our people by the control our representatives will have on the executive. Up till now, the executive was never made responsible to the Legislative Assembly and the Viceroy had the veto power, which rendered all the efforts of the elected members futile. Thanks to the efforts of the Swaraj Party, the Viceroy was forced every now and then to use these extraordinary powers to shamelessly trample the solemn decisions of the national representatives under foot. It is already too well known to need further discussion.

Now in the first place we must see the method of the executive formation: Whether the executive is to be elected by the members of a popular assembly or is to be imposed from above as before, and further, whether it shall be responsible to the house or shall absolutely affront it as in the past?

As regards the second item, we can judge it through the scope of franchise. The property qualifications making a man eligible to vote should be altogether abolished and universal suffrage be introduced instead. Every adult, both male and female, should have the right to vote. At present, we can simply see how far the franchise has been extended.

I may here make a mention about provincial autonomy. But from whatever I have heard, I can only say that the Governor imposed from above, equipped with extraordinary powers, higher and above the legislative, shall prove to be no less than a despot. Let us better call it the "provincial tyranny" instead of "autonomy". This is a strange type of democratisation of the state institutions.

The third item is quite clear. During the last two years, the British politicians have been trying to undo Montague's promise for another dole of reforms to be bestowed every ten years till the British Treasury exhausts.

We can see what they have decided about the future.

Let me make it clear that we do not analyse these things to rejoice over the achievement, but to form a clear idea about our situation, so that we may enlighten the masses and prepare them for further struggle. For us, compromise never means surrender, but a step forward and some rest. That is all and nothing else.

Having discussed the present situation, let us proceed to discuss the future programme and the line of action we ought to adopt. As I have already stated, for any revolutionary party, a definite programme is very essential. For, you must know that revolution means action. It means a change brought about deliberately by an organized and systematic work, as opposed to sudden and unorganised or spontaneous change or breakdown.

And for the formulation of a programme, one must necessarily study:

1. The goal.
2. The premises from where were to start, i.e. the existing conditions.
3. The course of action, i.e. the means and methods.

Unless one has a clear notion about these three factors, one cannot discuss anything about the programme.

We have discussed the present situation to some extent. The goal also has been slightly touched. We want a socialist revolution, the indispensable preliminary to which is the political revolution. That is what we want. The political revolution does not mean the transfer of state (or more crudely, the power) from the hands of the British to the Indian, but to those Indians who are one with us as to the final goal, or to be more precise, the power to be transferred to the revolutionary party through popular support. After that, to proceed in right earnest is to organize the reconstruction of the whole society on the socialist basis. If you do not mean this revolution, then please have mercy. Stop shouting "Long Live the Revolution". The term revolution is too sacred, at least to us, to be so lightly used or misused. But if you say you are for the national revolution and the aim of your struggle is an Indian republic of the type of the United State of America, then I ask you to please let known on what forces you rely that will help you bring about that revolution. Whether national or the socialist, are the peasantry and the labour. Congress leaders do not dare to organize those forces. You have seen it in this movement. They know it better than anybody else that without these forces, they are absolutely helpless. When they passed the resolution of complete independence - that really meant a revolution - they did not mean it. They had to do it under pressure of the younger element, and then they wanted to use it as a threat to achieve their hearts' desire - Dominion Status. You can easily judge it by studying the resolutions of the last three sessions of the Congress. I mean Madras, Calcutta and Lahore. At Calcutta, they passed a resolution asking for Dominion Status within twelve months, otherwise they would be forced to adopt complete independence as their object, and in all solemnity waited for some such gift till midnight after the 31st December, 1929. Then they found themselves "honour bound" to adopt the Independence resolution, otherwise they did not mean it. But even then, Mahatmaji made no secret of the fact that the door (for compromise) was open. That was the real spirit. At the very outset, they knew that their movement could not but end in some compromise. It is this half-heartedness that we hate, not the compromise at a particular stage in the struggle. Anyway, we were discussing the forces on which you can depend for a revolution. But if you say that you will approach the peasants and labourers to enlist their active support, let me tell you that they are not going to be fooled by any sentimental talk. They ask you quite candidly: what are they going to gain by your revolution for which you demand their sacrifices, what difference does it make to them whether Lord Reading is the head of the Indian government or Sir Purshotamdas Thakordas? What difference for a peasant if Sir Tej Bahadur Sapru replaces Lord Irwin! It is useless to appeal to his national sentiment. You can't "use" him for your purpose; you shall have to mean seriously and to make him understand that the revolution is going to be his and for his good. The revolution of the proletariat and *for* the proletariat.

When you have formulated this clear-cut idea about your goals, you can proceed in right earnest to organize your forces for such an action. Now there are two different phases through which you shall have to pass. First, the preparation; second, the action.

After the present movement ends, you will find disgust and some disappointment amongst the sincere revolutionary workers. But you need not worry. Leave sentimentalism aside. Be prepared to face the facts. Revolution is a very difficult task. It is beyond the power of any man to make a revolution. Neither can it be brought about on any appointed date. It is brought can it be brought about on an appointed date. It is brought about by special environments, social and economic. The function of an organized party is to utilise an such opportunity offered by these circumstances. And to prepare the masses and organize the forces for the revolution is a very difficult task. And that required a very great sacrifice on the part of the revolutionary workers.

Let me make it clear that if you are a businessman or an established worldly or family man, please don't play with fire. As a leader, you are of no use to the party. We have already very many such leaders who spare some evening hours for delivering speeches. They are useless. We require - to use the term so dear to Lenin - the "professional revolutionaries". The whole-time workers who have no other ambitions or life-work except the revolution. The greater the number of such workers organized into a party, the great the chances of your success.

To proceed systematically, what you need the most is a party with workers of the type discussed above, with clear-cut ideas and keen perception and ability of initiative and quick decisions. The party shall have iron discipline and it need not necessarily be an underground party rather the contrary. Though the policy of voluntarily going to jail should altogether be abandoned. That will create a number of workers who shall be forced to lead an underground life. They should carry on the work with the same zeal. And it is this group of workers that shall produce worthy leaders for the real opportunity.

The party requires workers which can be recruited only through the youth movement. Hence we find the youth movement as the starting point of our programme. The youth movement should organize study circles, class lectures and publication of leaflets, pamphlets, books and periodicals. This is the best recruiting and training ground for political workers.

Those young men who may have matured their ideas and may find themselves ready to devote their life to the cause, may be transferred to the party The party workers shall always guide and control the work of the

youth movement as well. The party should start with the
work of mass propaganda. It is very essential. One of the
fundamental causes of the failure of the efforts of the
Ghadar Party (1914-15) was the ignorance, apathy and
sometimes active opposition of the masses. And apart
from that, it is essential for gaining the active sympathy
of and of and organising the peasants and workers. This
party of political workers, bound by strict discipline,
should handle all other movements. It shall have to
organize the peasants' and workers' parties, labour unions,
and kindred political bodes. And in order to create
political consciousness, not only of national politics
but class politics as well, the party should organize a
big publishing campaign. Subjects on all proletens
enlightening the. masses of the socialist theory shall be
within easy reach and distributed widely The writings
should be simple and clear.

There are certain people in the labour movement who
enlist some absurd ideas about the economic liberty of
the peasants and workers without political freedom.
They are demagogues or muddle-headed people. Such
ideas are unimaginable and preposterous. We mean
the economic liberty of the masses, and for that very
purpose, we are striving to win the political power. No
doubt in the beginning, we shall have to fight for little
economic demands and privileges of these classes. But
these struggles are the best means for educating them for
a final struggle to conquer political power.

Apart from these, there shall necessarily be organized
a military department. This is very important. At times its
need is felt very badly. But at that time you cannot start
and formulate such a group with substantial means to

act effectively Perhaps this is the topic that needs careful explanation. There is very great probability of my being misunderstood on this subject. Apparently I have acted like a terrorist. But I am not a terrorist. I am a revolutionary who has got such definite ideas of a lengthy programme as is being discussed here. My "comrades in arms" might accuse me, like Ram Prasad Bismil, for having been subjected to certain sort of reaction in the condemned cell, which is not true. I have got the same ideas, same convictions, same zeal and same spirit as I used to have outside, perhaps -nay, decidedly - better. Hence I warn my readers to be careful while reading my words. They should not try to read anything between the lines. Let me announce with all the strength at my command, that I am not a terrorist and I never was, expected perhaps in the beginning of my revolutionary career. And I am convinced that we cannot gain anything through those methods. One can easily judge it from the history of the Hindustan Socialist Republican Association. All our activities were directed towards an aim, i.e. identifying ourselves with the great movement as its military wing. If anybody has misunderstood me, let him amend his ideas. I do not mean that bombs and pistols are useless, rather the contrary. But I mean to say that mere bomb-throwing is not only useless, but sometimes harmful. The military department of the party should always keep ready all the war-material it can command for any emergency, It should back the political work of the party. It cannot and should not work independently.

On these lines indicated above, the party should proceed with its work. Through periodical meetings and conferences, they should go on educating and enlightening their workers on all topics. If you start the work on these lines, you shall have to be very sober. The programme requires at least twenty years for its fulfillment. Cast aside the youthful dreams of a revolution within ten years, of Gandhis Utopian promises of Swaraj in one year. It requires neither the emotion nor the death, but the life of constant struggle, suffering and sacrifice. Crush your individuality first. Shake off the dreams of personal comfort. Then start to work. Inch by inch, you shall have to proceed. It needs courage, perseverance and very strong determination. No difficulties and no hardships shall discourage you. No failure and betrayals shall dishearten you. No travails (!) imposed upon you shall snuff out the revolutionary will in you. Through the ordeal of sufferings and sacrifice, you shall come out victorious. And these individual victories shall be the valuable assets of the revolution.

Long Live the Revolution!
2nd February, 1931

16

Line of Defence in Hari Kishan's Case

June, 1931

On 23 December 1930, when Governor of Punjab was leaving the University Hall, Lahore, after delivering his convocation address, Hari Kishan fired at him. One man died and the Governor was slightly injured. During the trial Hari Kishan's defence counsel took the line that Had Kishan had no intention to kill the Governor and that he only wanted to give a warning. Bhagat Singh was opposed to this line of defence. He wrote to one of his friends about how revolutionary cases should be conducted. This letter was later published in June 1931.

"My strength is the strength of oppressed; my courage is the courage of desperation."

- Bhagat Singh

I am very sorry to note that my last letter in this connection did not reach its destination at the proper time and therefore could be of no use, or failed to serve the purpose or which it was written. Hence, I write this letter to let you know my views on the question of defence in the political cases in general, and the revolutionary cases in particular. Apart from certain points already discussed in that letter, it shall serve another purpose too - it shall be a documentary proof that I am not becoming wise after the event.

Anyhow, I wrote in that letter that the plea that the lawyer was suggesting to offer defence, should not be adopted. But it has been done in spite of your and mine opposition. Nevertheless, we can now discuss the matter in a better light and can formulate definite ideas about the future policy regarding defence.

You know that I have never been in favour of defending all the political accused. But this does not imply that the beauty of the real struggle should be altogether spoiled. (Please note that the term beauty is not used in the abstract sense, but it means the motive that actuated a particular action.) When I say that all the politicals should always defend themselves, I say it with certain reservations. It can be cleared by just one explanation. A man does an act with a certain end in view. After his arrest, the political significance of the action should not be diminished. The perpetrator should not become more important than the action itself. Let us further elucidate it with the help of the illustration. Mr. Hari Kishan came to shoot the Governor. I don't want to discuss the ethical side of the action. I want only to discuss the political side of the case. The man was arrested. Unfortunately, some police official had died in the action. Now comes the question of the defence. Well, when fortunately the Governor had escaped there could be a very beautiful statement in his case, i.e. the statement of actual facts as was made in the lower court. And it would have served the legal purpose too. The wisdom and ability of the lawyer depended on his interpretation of the cause of the Sub-Inspectors death. What did he gain by saying that he did not intend to kill the Governor and only wanted to warn him, and all that sort of thing? Can any sensible man imagine even for a moment the possibility of such a design? Had it any legal value? Absolutely none. Then, what was the use of spoiling the beauty of not only the particular action but also the general movement? Warning and futile protests cannot go on forever. The warning has once been given long ago. The revolutionary struggle had begun in right earnest so far as the strength of the revolutionary party allowed. Viceroy's train action was neither a test, nor a warning. Similarly, Mr. Hari Kishan's action was part of the struggle itself, not a warning. After the failure of the action, the accused can take it in a sportman-like spirit. The purpose having been served, he ought to have rejoiced in the lucky escape of the Governor. There is no use of killing any one individual. These actions have their political significance in as much as they serve to create a mentality and an atmosphere which shall be very necessary to the final struggle. That is all. Individual actions are to win the moral support of the people. We sometimes designate them as 'propaganda through deed'.

Now, the people should be defended, but subject to the above consideration. This is, after all, a common principle that all the contending parties always try to gain more and lose less. No general can ever adopt a policy in which he may have to make a greater sacrifice than the gain expected. Nobody would be more anxious to save the precious life of Mr. Hari Kishan than myself. But I want to let you know that the thing which makes his life precious should by no means be ignored. To save the lives at any cost, is not our policy. It may be the policy of the easy-chair politicians, but it is not ours.

Much of the defence policy depends upon the mentality of the accused himself. But if the accused himself is not only afraid of shrinking, but is as enthusiastic as ever, than his work for which he risked his life should be considered first, his personal question afterwards. Again, there may be some sort of confusion. There may be cases where the action is of no general importance in spite of its tremendous local value. There the accused should not be sentimental as to admit the responsibility. The famous trial of Nirmal Kant Rai would be the best illustration.

But in cases like this, where it is of such political importance, the personal aspect should not be attached greater value than the political one. If you want to know my frank opinion about his case, let me tell you frankly, that it is nothing short of the political murder of an incident of historic importance at the altar of professional (legal) vanity.

Here I may point out one thing more, that the people responsible for this strangulation of the case, having realized their blunder and having become wise after the event in not daring to shoulder their responsibility, are trying to belittle the beauty of the marvellous character of our young comrade. I have heard them saying that Mr. Hari Kishan shirked to face it boldly.

This is a most shame-faced lie. He is the most courageous lad I have ever come across. People should have mercy upon us. Better ignored than demoralized and degraded but well looked after.

Lawyers should not be so unscrupulous as to exploit the one and even deaths of young people who come to sacrifice themselves for so noble a cause as the emancipation of the suffering humanity. I am really...[1], Otherwise, why should a lawyer demand such an incredible fee as has been paid in the above case?

In the sedition cases, I may tell you the limit to which we can allow the defence. Last year, when one comrade was prosecuted for having delivered a socialistic speech and when he pleaded not guilty to that charge, we were simply astounded. In such cases we should demand the right of free speech. But where such things are attributed to one as he has not said and are contrary to the interests of the movement, deny. Though in the present movement the Congress has suffered for having allowed its members to go to jail without defending themselves, in my opinion that was a mistake.

Anyhow, I think if you read this letter along with my previous one, you will come to know very clearly my ideas about the defence in political cases. In Mr. Hari Kishan's case, in my opinion, his appeal should be filed in the High Court without fail and every effort should be made to save him.

I hope both these letters indicate everything I want to say on this subject.

1 Some text missing from the original.

17

Introduction to 'The Dreamland'

When his friend Lala Ram Saran Das requested him to write an introduction to his collection of poems, Bhagat Singh penned down the following.

"Lovers, lunatics and poets are made of the same stuff."

- Bhagat Singh

My noble friend, L. Ram Saran Das, has asked me to write an introduction to his poetical work, 'The Dreamland'. I am neither a poet nor a literature, neither am I a journalist nor a critic. Hence, by no stretch of imagination can I find the justification of the demand. But the circumstances in which I am placed do not afford any opportunity of discussing the question with the author arguing back and forth, and thereby do not leave me any alternative but to comply with the desire of my friend.

As I am not a poet, I am not going to discuss it from that point of view. I have absolutely no knowledge of metre, and do not even know whether judged from metrical standard it would prove correct. Not being from literature I am not going to discuss it with a view of assigning to it its right place in the national literature.

I, being a political worker, can at the utmost discuss it only from that point of view. But here also, one factor is making my work practically impossible, or at least very difficult. As a rule, the introduction is always written by a man who is at one with the author on the contents of the work. But, here the case is quite different. I do not see eye to eye with my friend on all the matters. He was aware of the fact that I differed from him on many vital points. Therefore, my writing is not going to be an introduction at all. It can at the utmost amount to a criticism, and its place will be at the end and not in the beginning of the book.

In the political field, 'The Dreamland' occupies a very important place. In the prevailing circumstance, it is filling up a very important gap in the movement. As a matter of fact, all the political movements of our country that have hitherto played any important role in our modern history, had been lacking the ideal at the achievement of which they aimed. Revolutionary movement is no exception. In spite of all my efforts, I could not find any revolutionary party that had clear ideas as to what they were fighting for, with the exception of the Ghadar Party which, having been inspired by the USA form of government, clearly stated that they wanted to replace the existing government by a Republican form of government. All other parties consisted of men who had but one idea, i.e. to fight against the alien rulers. That idea is quite laudable, but cannot be termed a revolutionary idea. We must make it clear that revolution does not merely mean an upheaval or a sanguinary strife. Revolution necessarily implies the programme of systematic reconstruction of society on new and better adapted basis, after complete destruction of the existing state of affairs (i.e. regime).

In the political field, the liberals wanted some reform under the present government, while the extremists demanded a bit more and were prepared to employ radical means for the same purpose. Among the revolutionaries, they had always been in favour of extreme methods with one idea, i.e. of overthrowing the foreign domination. No doubt, there had been some who were in favour of extorting some reforms through those means. All these movements cannot rightly be designated as revolutionary movement.

But L. Ram Saran Das is the first revolutionary recruited formally in the Punjab by a Bengali absconder in 1908. Since then, he had been in touch with the revolutionary movements and finally joined the Ghadar Party, but retaining his old ideas that people held about the ideal of their movement. It has another interesting fact to add to its beauty and value. L. Ram Saran Das was sentenced to death in 1915, and the sentence was later on commuted to life transportation. Today, sitting in the condemned cells myself, I can let the readers know as authoritatively that the life imprisonment is comparatively a far harder lot than that of death. L. Ram Saran Das had actually to undergo fourteen years of imprisonment. It was in some southern jail that he wrote this poetry. The then psychology and mental struggle of the author has stamped its impressions upon the poetry and makes it all the more beautiful and interesting. He had been struggling hard against some depressing mood before he decided to write. In the days when many of his comrades had been let off on undertakings and the temptation had been very strong for everyone and for him, and when the sweet and painful memories of wife and children had added more to the work. Hence, we find the sudden outburst in the opening paragraph:

"Wife, children, friends that me surround
Were poisonous snakes all around."

He discusses philosophy in the beginning. This philosophy is the backbone of all the revolutionary movement of Bengal as well as of the Punjab. I differ from him on this point very widely. His interpretation of the universe is teleological and metaphysical, while I am a materialist and my interpretation of the phenomenon would be causal. Nevertheless, it is by no means out of place or out of date. The general ideals that are prevailing in our country are more in accordance with those expressed by him. To fight that depressing mood he resorted to prayers as is evident that the whole of the beginning of the book is devoted to god, his praise, his definition. Belief in god is the outcome of mysticism, which is the natural consequence of depression. That this world is *'maya'* or *'mithya'*, a dream or a fiction, is clear mysticism which has been originated and developed by Hindu sages of old ages, such as Shankaracharya and others. But in the materialist philosophy, this mode of thinking has got absolutely no place. But this mysticism of the author is by no means ignoble or deplorable. It has its own idea of them doing very productive labour. The only difference that the socialist society expects is that the mental workers shall no longer be regarded superior to the manual workers.

L. Ram Saran Das's idea about free education is really worth considering, and the socialist government has adopted somewhat the same course in Russia.

His discussion about crime is really the most advanced school of thought. Crime is the most serious social problem which needs a very tactful treatment. He has been in jail for the better part of his life. He has got the practical experience. At one place he employs the typical jail terms, 'the light labour, the medium labour and the hard labour', etc. Like all other socialists, he suggests that instead of retribution, i.e. retaliation, the reformative theory should form the basis of punishment. Not to punish but to reclaim should be the guiding principle of the administration of justice. Jails should be reformatories and not veritable hells. In this connection, the readers should study the Russian prison system.

While dealing with militia, he discusses war as well. In my opinion, war as an institution shall only occupy a few pages in the Encyclopaedia then, and war materials shall adorn the no conflicting or diverse interests that cause war.

At the utmost we can say that war shall have to be retained as an institution for the transitional period. We can easily understand if we take the example of the present-day Russia. There is the dictatorship of the proletariat at present. They want to establish a socialist society. Meanwhile they have to maintain an army to defend themselves against the capitalist society. But the war-aims would be different. Imperialist designs shall no more actuate our dreamland people to wage wars. There shall be no more war trophies. The revolutionary armies shall march to other lands, to bring rulers down from their thrones and stop their blood-sucking exploitation and thus to liberate the toiling masses. But, there shall not be the primitive national or racial hatred to goad our men to fight.

World-federation is the most popular and immediate object of all the free thinking people, and the author has well dilated on the subject, and his criticism of the so-called League of Nations is beautiful.

In a footnote under stanza 571 (572), the author touches, though briefly, the question of methods. He says: "Such a kingdom cannot be brought about by physical violent revolutions. It cannot be forced upon society from without. It must grow from within. This can be brought about by the gradual process of evolution, by educating the masses on the lines mentioned above", etc. This statement does not in itself contain any discrepancy. It is quite correct, but having not been fully explained, is liable to create some misunderstanding, or worse still, a confusion. Does it mean that L. Ram Saran Das has realised the futility of the cult of force? Has he become an orthodox believer in non-violence? No, it does not mean that.

Let me explain what the above quoted statement amounts to. The revolutionaries know better than anybody else that the socialist society cannot be brought about by violent means, but that it should grow and evolve from whitin. The author suggests education as the only weapon to be employed. But, everybody can easily realise that the present government here, or, as a matter of fact, all the capitalist governments are not only not going to help any such effort, but on the contrary, suppress it mercilessly. Then, what will his 'evolution' achieve? We the revolutionaries are striving to capture power in our hands and to organize a revolutionary government which should employ all its resources for mass education, as is being done in Russia today. After capturing power, peaceful methods shall be employed for constructive work, force shall be employed to crush the obstacles. If that is what the author means, then we are at one. And I am confidant that it is exactly this that he means.

I have discussed the book at great length. I have rather criticised it. But, I am not going to ask any alteration in it, because this has got its historical value. These were the ideas of 1914-15 revolutionaries.

I strongly recommend this book to young men in particular, but with a warning. Please do not read it to follow blindly and take for granted what is written in it. Read it, criticise it, think over it, and try to formulate your own ideas with its help.

18

Don't Hang Us; Shoot Us

1931

Bhagat Singh's last letter of petition to expedite the order of his execution.

"I am such a lunatic that I am free even in jail."

- Bhagat Singh

To:

The Punjab Governor

Sir,

With due respect, we beg to bring to your kind notice the following: That we were sentenced to death on 7th October 1930 by a British Court, LCC Tribunal, constituted under the Sp. Lahore Conspiracy Case Ordinance, promulgated by the H.E. The Viceroy, the Head of the British Government of India, and that the main charge against us was that of having waged war against H.M. King George, the King of England.

The above-mentioned finding of the Court pre-supposed two things:

Firstly, that there exists a state of war between the British Nation and the Indian Nation and, secondly, that we had actually participated in that war and were therefore war prisoners.

The second pre-supposition seems to be a little bit flattering, but nevertheless, it is too tempting to resist the desire of acquiescing in it.

As regards the first, we are constrained to go into some detail. Apparently there seems to be no such war as the phrase indicates. Nevertheless, please allow us to accept the validity of the presupposition taking it at its face value. But in order to be correctly understood, we must explain it further. Let us declare that the state of war does exist and shall exist so long as the Indian toiling masses and the natural resources are being exploited by a handful of parasites. They may be purely British Capitalist or mixed British and Indian or even purely Indian. They may be carrying on their insidious exploitation through mixed or even on purely Indian bureaucratic apparatus. All these things make no difference. No matter, if your government tries and succeeds in winning over the leaders of the upper strata of the Indian Society through petty concessions and compromises, and thereby cause a temporary demoralization in the main body of the forces. No matter, if once again the vanguard of the Indian movement, the Revolutionary Party, finds itself deserted in the thick of the war. No matter if the leaders to whom personally we are much indebted for the sympathy and feelings they expressed for us, but nevertheless we cannot overlook the fact that they did become so callous as to ignore and not to make a mention in the peace negotiation of even the homeless, friendless and penniless of female workers who are alleged to be belonging to the vanguard and whom the leaders consider to be enemies of their Utopian non-violent cult which has already become a thing of the past; the heroines who had ungrudgingly sacrificed or offered for sacrifice their husbands, brothers, and all that were nearest and dearest to them, including themselves, whom your government has declared to be outlaws. No matter, it your agents stoop so low as to fabricate baseless calumnies against their spotless characters to damage their and their party's reputation. The war shall continue.

It may assume different shapes at different times. It may become now open, now hidden, now purely agitational, now fierce life and death struggle. The choice of the course, whether bloody or comparatively peaceful, which it should adopt rests with you. Choose whichever you like. But that war shall be incessantly waged without taking into consideration the petty and the meaningless ethical ideologies. It shall be waged ever with new vigour, greater audacity and unflinching determination till the Socialist Republic is established and the present social order is completely replaced by a new social order, based on social prosperity and thus every sort of exploitation is put an end to and the humanity is ushered into the era of genuine and permanent peace. In the very near future, the final battle shall be fought and final settlement arrived at.

The days of capitalist and imperialist exploitation are numbered. The war neither began with us, nor is it going to end with our lives. It is the inevitable consequence of the historic events and the existing environments. Our humble sacrifices shall be only a link in the chain that has very accurately been beautified by the unparalleled sacrifice of Mr. Das and most tragic but noblest sacrifice of Comrade Bhagawati Charan and the glorious death of our dear warrior Azad.

As to the question of our fates, please allow us to say that when you have decided to put us to death, you will certainly do it. You have got the power in your hands and power is the greatest justification in this world. We know that the maxim "Might is right" serves as your guiding motto. The whole of our trial was just a proof of that. We wanted to point out that according to the verdict of your court, we had waged war and were therefore war prisoners. And we claim to be treated as such, i.e. we claim to be shot dead instead of to be hanged. It rests with you to prove that you really meant what your court has said.

We request and hope that you will very kindly order the military department to send its detachment to perform our execution.

Yours,
Bhagat Singh

Scan QR code to access the
Penguin Random House India website